Understanding Behaviour in Early Years Settings

Everything we learn, every way we influence others and every relationship we form hangs around a complex interplay of behaviours, feelings and thoughts. This practical book explores the factors that influence children's behaviour in the early years, enabling practitioners, parents and carers to develop a better understanding and become more intuitive and confident in supporting their development and learning in the first five years.

Full of insights and strategies for supporting children when their behaviour gets in the way of learning and wellbeing, or when it is simply 'different' in some way, Understanding Behaviour in Early Years Settings demonstrates how practitioners can help children to feel secure, learn and explore while gaining an understanding of how to behave socially and appropriately towards others. Areas covered include

- building firm foundations and developing attachments;
- personal, social and emotional development;
- the language of feelings and behaviour;
- observing 'problem' behaviours and planning interventions; and
- supporting disability and special educational needs.

Including case studies and thinking points in each chapter, this invaluable guide will help early years practitioners, teachers and students to develop their own knowledge, confidence and understanding when working with challenging behaviours.

Hannah Mortimer is an independent educational psychologist in the UK and has published over 60 books on early years education, child development and special educational needs.

Understanding Behaviour in Early Years Settings

Supporting Personal, Social and Emotional Development from 0–5

Hannah Mortimer

Routledge
Taylor & Francis Group
LONDON AND NEW YORK

First published 2017
by Routledge
2 Park Square, Milton Park, Abingdon, Oxon OX14 4RN

and by Routledge
711 Third Avenue, New York, NY 10017

Routledge is an imprint of the Taylor & Francis Group, an informa business

© 2017 Hannah Mortimer

The right of Hannah Mortimer to be identified as author of this work has been asserted by her in accordance with sections 77 and 78 of the Copyright, Designs and Patents Act 1988.

All rights reserved. No part of this book may be reprinted or reproduced or utilised in any form or by any electronic, mechanical, or other means, now known or hereafter invented, including photocopying and recording, or in any information storage or retrieval system, without permission in writing from the publishers.

Trademark notice: Product or corporate names may be trademarks or registered trademarks, and are used only for identification and explanation without intent to infringe.

British Library Cataloguing in Publication Data
A catalogue record for this book is available from the British Library

Library of Congress Cataloguing in Publication Data
Names: Mortimer, Hannah.
Title: Understanding behaviour in early years settings : supporting personal, social and emotional development from 0-5 / Hannah Mortimer.
Description: New York : Routledge, 2017.
Identifiers: LCCN 2016042576 | ISBN 9781138233997 (hardback) | ISBN 9781138234000 (pbk.) | ISBN 9781315308234 (ebook)
Subjects: LCSH: Behavior modification. | Child psychology. | Child psychology—Social aspects.
Classification: LCC LB1060.2 .M67 2017 | DDC 371.102/4—dc23
LC record available at https://lccn.loc.gov/2016042576

ISBN: 978-1-138-23399-7 (hbk)
ISBN: 978-1-138-23400-0 (pbk)
ISBN: 978-1-315-30823-4 (ebk)

Typeset in Optima
by diacriTech, Chennai

For Garry

Contents

	Acknowledgements	ix
	Introduction	xi
1	**Firm foundations: Attachments and beginnings**	1
2	**Personal and social development: Fitting in and making friends**	15
3	**Emotional development: Feeling good, behaving well**	28
4	**The language of behaviour: Words, thoughts and metaphors**	40
5	**Environmental factors: Expectations, reactions and creating the right ethos**	51
6	**When behaviour needs to change: Observations and planning interventions**	67
7	**Children who behave 'differently': Special educational needs and disability**	86
8	**Supporting parents, carers and each other**	104
	Further information	120
	Index	121

Acknowledgements

Some of the practical approaches and pen pictures throughout this book are adapted from two of my previous publications by QEd, *Behaviour Management in the Early Years* and *An A-Z of Tricky Behaviours in the Early Years*. I am grateful to Colin Gallow for permission to do so. Acknowledgements to Alison Knights for sharing her wealth of information on strengths-based approaches and early neurological development, and to Tink Palmer for her continuing inspiration and wisdom. Thank you to Karen Bibbings for 'the Glums' activity on page 5. Above all, acknowledgements and thanks are due to the children, families and colleagues whom I have had the privilege of working with in the Tees Valley and North Yorkshire for the past forty years.

Introduction

There is no separating our behaviour from everything we are and everything we do – as we live and breathe, so do we behave. In a social world, our behaviour is noticed, responded to and influenced by those around us and whole social worlds are created for us to inhabit. Everything we learn, every way we influence others and every relationship we form hangs around a complex interplay of behaviours, feelings and thoughts. What a simply brilliant subject for a book on early years! If we could but crack the code, how effective we could be as early years practitioners; but, of course, it is never that simple.

This book aims to explore the factors that influence children's behaviour in their first five years. It aims to do so in a practical way, linking what we know into what we can do to support the children we live and work with. The rationale goes that if practitioners, parents and carers can develop a better understanding of why children behave as they do, they can become more confident and intuitive when supporting children's development and learning. In doing so, they can help each child to feel secure, to explore and learn, and to behave socially and appropriately towards others.

There are two broad themes:

- Why children behave as they do and how to support their personal and social development
- How to plan positive and child-centred interventions when behaviour becomes inappropriate or 'different' in some way

Throughout the book, there will be boxed sections which will be helpful for reflection and in-service training:

- *Thinking points*, with a scenario and questions
- *Pen pictures* of children whose behaviour was causing concern in the setting, what staff did and why their intervention was effective

Introduction

These scenarios are adapted from real examples in my experience as an early years educational psychologist. They are adapted with acknowledgements from my book *An A–Z of Tricky Behaviours in the Early Years* (Mortimer 2006).

Throughout the book, I will simplify the language by using the term 'practitioner' to represent any early years professional working within a setting or childminding situation. Because I am trying to avoid quoting typical ages to accompany the developmental stages we cover, I will use the general terms 'babies,' 'toddlers' and 'young children', referring always to children from nought to five.

The broad canvas

The book aims to explore how an understanding of why children behave as they do can inspire the learning opportunities we create for them. We look at how children's social and emotional behaviour typically develops from birth to five years and then explore how early years practitioners can apply this knowledge in order to understand why children behave as they do. There are insights and strategies for supporting children when their behaviour gets in the way of learning and well-being, or when it is simply different in some way. We look at children who have additional needs associated with social, emotional and mental health difficulties and therefore require approaches that are additional or different to usual. For these children, we explore what an *individual behaviour plan* might look like for planning and evaluating your interventions. We will be encouraged to move away from following set recipes for dealing with set behaviours and move instead towards becoming 'behaviour detectives'. The book also explores our own feelings and potential stresses when working with challenging behaviour and how we can support each other, parents and carers.

Who the book is aimed at

The book will be of interest to early years practitioners and teachers in a wide range of settings, including childminders, voluntary organisations, schools and trainees. Early years trainers and managers should find it a useful resource for initial training, for staff development and for designing whole-setting approaches. Early years special educational needs coordinators (SENCOs) and support staff will find suggestions for assessment and intervention for young children with additional needs in a format which can be shared with colleagues. Whilst written mainly with a professional audience in mind, children's behaviour is children's behaviour, and, as such, the approaches and ways of exploring behaviour will also be of interest to parents and carers who wish to understand more about why children in social groups behave in the way that they do over their first five years.

Introduction

Working within frameworks

We live in times of rapid change and this book does not attempt to quote the latest statutory guidance and the various frameworks under which we operate within the early years sector. There are contact details for the main government departments in the Further information section at the end of the book. Instead, the main body of the book focuses on how children's behaviour typically develops within the first five years and what influences it. In this way, the information and practical suggestions should remain relevant and current for readers living and working in different countries.

Guiding principles

It helps if you and your colleagues share some basic principles and visions concerning your work with young children's behaviour. Here are some examples (adapted from Drummond, Rouse and Pugh, 1992).

- We encourage the children to behave appropriately using positive approaches which encourage their self-esteem.
- We manage the children's behaviour with a proper respect for the children themselves and their parents or carers. We respect their culture, their ethnicity, their language, their religion, their age and their gender. The approaches we use for managing behaviour must be respectful of all children regardless of their gifts, abilities or specific learning needs.
- Behaviour management and the personal, social and emotional education of young children are not two separate, discrete activities. As a consequence, when we work with young children's behaviour, we will attend to their whole development and lives and not to certain aspects of it.
- We believe in the principle of the *loving use of power*. Early years educators inevitably have power; this needs to be acknowledged and used lovingly, wisely and well.
- The interests of the child are paramount. Changing their behaviour must enhance their lives, their learning and their development. It must work for the child.
- We also recognise that children will thrive best only if their families thrive, and we aim to work in close partnership with families and the community.

How the book is organised and how to use it

You will find it best to read through the whole book first, since one chapter builds on the explorations and insights of the previous one. Having done so, it would be possible to dip into the interventions and approaches in your daily work. The chapters are organised in this way.

Chapter 1 explores how we plan firm foundations for the babies and toddlers in our care. There is an introduction to attachment theory in simple terms and why its understanding is so basic to how we respond to children's behaviour. Understanding a little about what happens when attachments go wrong has implications for how we support the children in our care and allows us to distinguish challenging behaviour from challenging children. We explore some exciting new developments in what we know about brain development and how this leads us to working with children's strengths in order to support their behaviour and well-being. If we can learn to tune in to the child as a unique individual and learn to listen to their behaviours, we can then plan an ethos of security in which the child can explore and socialise.

In Chapter 2, we begin to look at how children typically develop personal and social skills, thinking in terms of stages rather than ages, since these vary so widely. We look at typical stages young children go through when learning to fit in and make friends and begin to see the importance of seeing young children's behaviour through a developmental lens. This will provide you with a framework for monitoring development, observation and celebrating those 'ta-da!' moments when you can almost see children's connections and learning taking place before your very eyes. We also hear about the use of musical circle times to promote children's social skills and behaviour.

Chapter 3 focuses on emotional development, linking this to behaviour; this can be summed up as, 'feeling good, behaving well'. Building on what we learned in Chapter 1, we explore the links between self-esteem, self-confidence and learning. This enables us to see the importance of nurturing and key working, and of having clear rules, routines and boundaries to engender feelings of security. We look at ideas for building children's confidence within the setting. We also explore how to support children who have gone through major life changes or trauma, their typical emotional reactions and how to support these.

It is worth devoting a chapter to the language of behaviour and this is covered in Chapter 4. We reflect on the language we use to describe behaviour and how this influences the way we respond to it. We look at ideas for helping children develop the words they need to express their feelings. There are also creative examples of using stories, resources and metaphors to help children learn about feelings and behaviours.

Chapter 5 looks at environmental factors which affect children's behaviour such as their surroundings, their internal states, the expectations and reactions of others and creating the right ethos. Armed with what we know from the earlier chapters, we begin to develop our skills as behaviour detectives. We are encouraged to investigate what we believe is keeping a particular behaviour going and how we might influence it. Environmental factors and triggers that influence behaviour can be both internal (such as diet, sleep, temperament) and external (such as cause-and-effect, management styles, personal history). This leads us on to explore the transitions that children might find tricky and how to plan for them. Once we have thought about how we can create the right environment for positive behaviour and emotional well-being, we can capture this in our 'behaviour policy'.

Sometimes our usual approaches and nurturing environments do not seem to be effective for a child. Chapter 6 looks at those situations when inappropriate behaviour needs to change, with observations and practical ideas for planning interventions. When does a behaviour become a 'problem', and for whom is it a problem? There is an introduction to behaviour management in a positive, practical and child-centred way. We also look at planning special educational needs approaches which are *additional* and *different* than usual and how to record these on an individual behaviour plan. To support each other when planning behavioural change, a format for a consultative approach within the setting is described. Rather than follow a 'cookbook' recipe for changing a child's behaviour, we are encouraged to develop our own recipe for behavioural change.

There will be some children in your care who follow a different pathway in their development and behaviour because of a learning difficulty or disability, and these children are introduced in Chapter 7. We explore the pros and cons of labelling behaviour difficulties and when it becomes important to plan SEND *(special educational needs and disabilities)* approaches which are additional or different to usual. Children with autistic spectrum disorders may learn and behave differently, and there are many practical strategies for understanding and working with this. We also look at children who have significant attention difficulties, with an emphasis on creative and individual planning and inclusion rather than spotting something being 'wrong'.

Finally, there are suggestions for how to support parents, carers and each other in Chapter 8. Handling times when children's behaviour is challenging can be stressful for everyone, and this needs to be acknowledged and supported as well. Sometimes we need to understand our own emotional luggage when it comes to working with challenging behaviours. We also need to develop our understanding of where parents who are carers are 'coming from' and how to listen and support them when discussing their young children's behaviour. We look at sharing behaviour plans between home and setting, with an emphasis on empowering rather than deskilling. Finally, there are further contacts sources of information at the end of the book.

References

Drummond, M. J., Rouse, D. and Pugh, G. (1992) *Making Assessment Work: Values and Principles in Assessing Young Children's Learning.* London: National Children's Bureau and Nottingham: NES Arnold.

Mortimer, H. (2006) *An A–Z of Tricky Behaviours in the Early Years*. Stafford: QEd Publications.

Firm foundations: Attachments and beginnings

The first chapter is all about beginnings; both behaviour during a baby's first months of life, though also first principles in terms of understanding early emotional development. We explore exciting new developments in what we are learning about neurological development. We also look at the importance of developing secure attachments in the early years and how this should inform all of our planning and support. Understanding more about these two areas – early brain development and the formation of attachments – can give us a framework for understanding why babies, toddlers and young children behave and feel as they do and what we, in turn, can do to support them.

We will start this chapter by unpacking what we know so far, and then weave the implications into our explorations throughout the rest of the book, with an emphasis on working with children's strengths rather than their challenges. *Strengths-based approaches* concentrate on the inherent strengths of individuals, families, groups and organisations, deploying personal strengths to promote development, aid recovery and empower. In essence, when we focus on health and well-being, we embrace an asset-based approach where the goal is to promote the positive rather than to emphasise the negative.

The developing brain

In her book *What Every Parent Needs to Know* (2007), Margot Sunderland paints a picture of the remarkable effects of love, nurture and play on a child's brain development and behaviour. Our brains have evolved over millions of years and consist of three regions, each with its own function and linked to the others by a massive network of connections.

We each have a

- core reptilian brain situated deep and activating instinctive behaviours related to survival, such as hunger, breathing, temperature control, movement and primitive *fight-or-flight* reactions;

- a lower mammalian brain, or *limbic system*, regulating rage, fear, separation distress, caring and nurturing, social bonding, playfulness, and the urge to explore; and
- a higher human brain (or 'rational brain') situated in the frontal lobes and responsible for problem-solving, reasoning and reflection, self-awareness, creativity and imagination and higher emotional behaviours such as kindness, empathy and concern.

Much of the infant's brain develops after birth and this is why it is so susceptible to styles of parenting and care. When born, a baby has around 200 billion brain cells, but very few of those in the higher brain (which actually constitutes 85% of the brain's total mass) have actually become connected. So you can see that babies are born with all the ingredients there but their brains are as yet 'uncooked', as it were. Learning and development basically requires making connections between our brain cells, and there are critical periods of brain growth in the first five years. In fact, 90% of the growth of the human brain occurs in the first five years of life.

Because the child's higher brain is so unfinished, it is inevitable that young children's behaviour will be dominated by the emotional and primitive areas of the brain – there will be times when they appear to be all feelings and reactions. When strong feelings of rage, fear or separation distress overwhelm children, they need our compassion, soothing and physical comfort to be calmed so that their dysregulated body and brain systems are brought back into balance. Without this emotional responsiveness, the brain might never develop the pathways needed to cope with stress and strong emotions later in life. This one piece of knowledge should fundamentally change the way we view babies' and toddlers' behaviour; as parents, practitioners and carers, we need to read the feelings and not simply manage the behaviour.

Why babies cry

If we are going to explore behaviour from the earliest age, then we must begin with crying behaviour. All young mammals are programmed to cry as a way of communicating their need for help. This makes crying a totally normal part of the baby's life. Babies cry for many different reasons: hunger, tiredness, overstimulation, discomfort or separation – in fact, in response to the sheer nature and shock of the unpredictable world they have arrived in. Though it is hard at first to work out what their crying means, this becomes easier in time as a parent or dedicated carer becomes tuned in to their signals.

Crying usually peaks at around six weeks and then abates at around 12 to 16 weeks. After this time, older babies and toddlers will cry when they are cold, hungry, tired, ill or bored. Before words develop, crying is the baby's only means of saying no and letting us hear their choices. For example, a baby who cries when passed to someone new might be telling you, 'No, I don't want you to pass me to someone else as I was so comfortable in your arms and I'm not sure about their unfamiliar smell'.

Crying in itself does not affect a baby's developing brain – it is all part of the normal signalling system. However, prolonged and intense crying representing uncomforted and frightening stress, can be harmful. If left to cry like this for too often, a stress response system in the brain may be affected for life and this explains some of what we are seeing when we look at the behaviour of children who lack positive attachments (see 'Patterns of attachment' later). When children cry in an intense, desperate way, their whole bodily arousal system is out of balance. Their whole body is primed for fight or flight reaction, with high levels of adrenaline, higher blood pressure and faster heart rate. Prolonged arousal and stress can lead to the body and brain becoming hardwired for *hyperarousal*, with various symptoms of stress throughout life.

Many of us simply do not realise that a baby's bodily arousal system is still developing after birth and that soothing and calming really are essential parts of the care that we give. You can begin to see why it is so important to have a dedicated key person who knows a baby or young child well enough to interpret their signals and tune in to what they need from you. 'Good enough' caring is simply not good enough for a baby's healthy emotional development. Babies need the security of someone who knows their signals well, knows how to sooth and comfort them and can pitch the level of sensory stimulation at just the right level for the baby's arousal system.

It is fascinating that, even with young babies, one can begin to see different patterns emerging in how much stimulation is 'just right' for each of them. This makes it so important for us to tune in to them before we make assumptions that an 'all singing and dancing' approach will be right for everyone. Some babies quickly become bored and need a higher level of input. Some startle very easily and become overloaded with stimulation; each is unique. Already we are beginning to see that understanding and working with young children's behaviour is part and parcel of becoming a behaviour detective and tuning into what makes each child individual and responsive.

Thinking point: How good are we at listening to babies' behaviour?

We know that we must tune in to babies and young children if we are to support their attachments and emotional development. Whilst most of us can visualise how we might observe and tune in to older children's behaviour, it is more challenging for us to think about *listening* to what babies are telling us through their behaviour. When it comes to babies, we can consider these four strands:

- Communicating effectively: Babies communicate all the time through their sounds, movement, actions and signals. Do we 'hear' and respond to these whenever appropriate?
- Encouraging participation: Our role becomes one of making sure that all can participate in what we have to offer. Do we offer a broad and balanced session? Do we help each baby to take part and feel cared for and successful?

(Continued)

(Continued)

- Tuning in: Are we good at tuning in to babies as individuals, recognising and interpreting their early communication? Can anyone do this, or does it take a key person who knows the baby well?
- Offering choices: Do we understand that babies have their own priorities, interests, concerns and rights too? Do we offer choices so that each baby's individual needs and interests are met? In other words, how flexible are we able to be?

Attachment theory in simple terms

We have been thinking about how early nurturing and stimulation can affect the baby's later emotional development. The ability to tune in appears to be central in promoting healthy attachments. Attachment theory argues that children develop a style of relating to important attachment figures in their lives which secures for them the best parenting or caring available under the circumstances. The study of attachments has opened up a whole new way of planning our care, assessing relationships and providing therapeutic support when things have gone wrong.

Function of attachment

We know of the importance of secure, healthy attachments from the work of John Bowlby and colleagues (1998). The purpose of healthy attachments includes the following:

- They ensure the child's need for safety, protection and sense of security.
- Proximity seeking and exploratory behaviour are balanced at each developmental stage to maximise the child's development.
- A healthy attachment becomes activated by threat and so ensures protection.
- The quality of attachment is related to how well parents or carers can tune in to the child, and so qualities in the caregiver or carer (and that includes early years practitioners) can affect it both positively and negatively.
- Through the pattern of attachment, growing children develop internal working models in their brains, which form the basis of personal-social development and how relationships are formed in the future.
- Secure attachment is a protective factor for positive mental health in later life.

From research (and there is a useful summary in Read, 2014), we now know more about patterns of attachment between parents and their children, and we can begin to identify those who are successfully connected or bonded from those who are not. Here is a simple activity to explain what connection looks like.

> **Thinking point: The Glums**
>
> Imagine you are sitting in a restaurant. In one corner, there is a couple who are obviously deeply in love. We will call them the Lovers. How do you *know* that they are in love – what behaviours do you actually observe? Make a list of these on a large sheet of paper.
>
> Now imagine you are in the same restaurant and in another corner is a couple who are clearly not getting on very well. We will call them the Glums. What do you actually see or hear this time? Make another list.
>
> Things to consider:
>
> - Think about parents or carers and children who are attached or connected to each other – do you observe similar behaviours as the Lovers and the Glums?
> - You now know what a *connected* child and carer look like. Can you also recognise when such a connection is *not* there?
> - Think of ways you can support attachments/connections by helping parents or carers tune in to their children and to share pleasure in each other.

Patterns of attachment

The patterns of attachment remain remarkably consistent over time until the child is about six, and so can be observed, identified and worked with. There are some children whose challenging behaviour is very resistant to change. These are the children who can settle better if given secure attachment figures (such as a dedicated key person) to relate to who can support, offer consistency of handling, and be there to reassure, encourage and champion the child. They also respond best to the secure base of a familiar setting, routines and familiar faces. Parents and carers of children with attachment difficulties may find that their children are difficult to control, extremely angry and aggressive, very withdrawn or highly anxious and 'clingy' for much longer than is usual.

How can we understand these patterns? If a parent is unresponsive or rejecting of a baby's cries of distress, that child may act as if he or she is independent long before being emotionally ready to be independent. Such children may pay little attention when their parents leave them at nursery, and seldom look at their parents or try to involve them in their play. This is known as a pattern of *anxious-avoidant attachment*. If parents are inconsistent in their responses, perhaps because of periods of depression, emotional detachment or separation, their children learn to cry or shout louder with their demands, producing a pattern of *ambivalent attachment*. There is also a pattern of *disorganized or controlling attachment* in which children develop a very controlling style over their parents in order to maintain some degree of predictability or structure. This pattern is common with parents who might have suffered loss, trauma or abuse themselves or who lack a secure base of their own from which to provide nurture and care to others in their lives.

Where there are attachment difficulties, you might notice that the child finds it difficult to receive genuine positive attention ('She doesn't respond to praise'), and you might see destructive behaviour with themselves, with possessions, or with their own creations ('As soon as I praise his model, he destroys it'). There might be a superficial affection with strangers ('She'll go with anyone'). Sometimes you see a stealing or hoarding of food or desired objects with a difficulty in telling the truth, even if it is obvious that it is a lie. There might be problems with friendships because of over-controlling behaviour and poor eye contact when a parent or carer tries to address issues with them. Understanding about attachments does not mean that we should go forth and proclaim that a parent or child has an attachment disorder. However, it does help us to understand that there is an emotional component to the behaviour or the relationship which may involve us trying to intervene on an emotional level as well as a behavioural or teaching level.

Risk and resilience

There are a number of risk factors for children making them more likely to experience behavioural difficulties or mental health problems later on:

- Loss or separation, perhaps because someone in their family has died, their parents or caregivers have split up, there has been a long period in hospital or there have been many changes of home and caregivers
- Major life changes, such as becoming a refugee, moving house or changing families ('looked after' children are particularly vulnerable)
- Traumatic events, such as violence, accidents, injuries, war, natural disaster or abuse
- Having a 'difficult temperament' or a very low self-esteem, perhaps not being flexible enough to adapt to different social situations
- Having learning or communication difficulties
- Socio-economic disadvantage and homelessness

Whilst many children with many of these risk factors will grow and develop with no mental health problems whatsoever, risk factors do seem to stack up. Try not to judge a child's behaviour – you might not have the full picture of why he or she is behaving in a certain way, and any unhelpful labelling could suggest that the behaviour is somehow fixed and cannot be changed.

Forming positive attachments in the setting

Young children can learn to form secure attachments within the setting through your consistency and nurturing. This works best if you understand how attachments work and ensure you have consistency of nurturing and care. When children are 'stuck' in a certain pattern of behaving because of an attachment difficulty, they have become stuck in a kind of battle game. There is an apparent need for the child to be in control of everything, they tend to see everything as win or lose, and they 'win' if they do not do as the carer requests or if they make carers angry. What they may be doing is trying to re-create the early chaos in their own lives. Your best approaches will be your unconditional calmness, consistency, and ability to let the child know that you can understand and contain their strong feelings.

Useful strategies

Here are some general strategies which will help you to develop positive attachments within your setting (adapted from Mortimer, 2006):

- Use of the key person, acting as a secure base for the child
- Use of comforters and favourite cuddly toys
- Tuning in to the individual baby or child; 'listening' to their behaviours
- Narratives which make the child feel special ('When you were first started nursery, you loved the water tray and you were so excited when …')
- Celebrating babyhood – saving early photos and life stories
- Seeing these young children through the lens of their early neurological development
- Not being frightened or alarmed by a child's reactions and behaviour, and remaining calm
- Enjoying warm, appropriate physical contact together
- Aiming for high warmth, low criticism
- Calming the 'battle' and not adding anger to anger
- Making the most of good support networks yourself as you might be finding this work particularly challenging (there is more about this in Chapter 8)
- Ensuring calm, predictable daily routines
- Planning ahead to get through the session
- Helping parents and other carers to tune in to what it was like when *they* were little
- Sharing fun together with the baby or child

You could also consider planning a 'special playtime', considering running a 'relationship circle' or setting up a 'nurture corner'. These are three simple interventions which can be planned within the setting to promote positive attachments for any children you have concerns about. *Special playtime* is a one-to-one intervention for helping a key person and child become more tuned in to each other, or for sharing with a parent for him or her to use at home. *The relationship circle* is a group approach involving adult-child pairs. *Nurture corners* are something you can set up as part of your environment to serve as secure bases for those children who need extra settling and reassurance.

Special playtime

This is a simple intervention that can be used by a key person, or can be shared with a parent, to positively influence attachment. If you are working with parents, hand out a copy of the guidelines and talk them through. Explain that is has been shown to make a parent and child feel more connected, and that this will help the child's behaviour. Practise it together with the child (it tends not to happen otherwise), and follow it up weekly for a while.

Special playtime

1. Set a definite time for 10 minutes' special play with your child every day.
2. Ask your child to decide what he or she wants to play with – perhaps offer a box of toys so your child can chose something.
3. Agree on an activity you will do – playing with the cars perhaps or sharing a picture book.
4. Join in wholeheartedly.
5. Give a running commentary on what your child is doing – 'Oh – you've got the big truck – it's going into the shed now … here it comes'. It shows your child you are interested in what he or she doing.
6. Add positive comments like 'I enjoy playing cars with you'.
7. Praise your child repeatedly.
8. There should be no criticism at all, and don't say no – if you have to correct your child, say what to do instead.
9. Laugh together and enjoy rough-and-tumble play or hugs as you share the fun.
10. Finish by talking about what you have done together and how you enjoyed it.

Relationship circle

One of the ways in which professionals can work with children who need support to develop positive attachments is through *relationship play*. We adapted some of these ideas in a 'Hugs and Tugs' group that we ran within a nursery setting for parents and carers of selected children. Along with the other ideas we have explored within this chapter, we wanted to provide a therapeutic intervention for some of the children we were concerned about. We sometimes used this for key person and child pairs and sometimes worked with health visitors, inviting parents or home carers so that they could be supported in their individual relationship with the child.

We sat in a circle on the floor, making sure that each child was sitting next to or cuddled into their parent or key person. We then ran a ten- to fifteen-minute relationship circle time, starting with non-threatening activities that did not place demands on a carer and child through having to relate too closely. In the early sessions, activities tended to involve little touch or eye contact. We then progressed over about ten sessions to activities and action rhymes that involve closer contact, more interaction and a sharing of pleasure and fun together. The activities below are just some examples of how you can adapt familiar action games and rhymes so that they are graded from the least physical and emotional involvement to the most.

Getting started: Action rhymes for the relationship circle

Starting off

Break the ice by singing a familiar song to start with. Keep this song the same throughout the sessions to provide a sense of security. We chose 'The Wheels on the Bus', since everyone knew it and we could vary the verses from the impersonal ('the wheels on the bus go round and round') to the more intimate ('the horn on the bus goes beep beep beep' with adults gently pushing 'their' child's nose). Towards the end of the sessions, we had 'the mums on the bus go cuddle cuddle cuddle' or 'tickle tickle tickle', and we also had children pretending to be babies and cuddling into their adults for 'the babies on the bus fall fast asleep'. Thus in one rhyme, you can see the whole progression of the relationship circle!

Row, row

This is another action rhyme which allowed us various stages of physical contact. Sing the familiar rhyme:

> Row, row, row your boat, gently down the stream,
> Merrily, merrily, merrily, merrily, life is but a dream.

In the earlier sessions, children had their backs to their adults who sang this in a circle as they gently rocked the children. Towards the end, we had adults and children facing each other and sharing fun. Try changing the last line for introducing feelings:

> If you see a crocodile, don't forget to scream!
> If you see a tall giraffe, don't forget to laugh!

(Continued)

(Continued)

> If you see a hippopotamus, don't forget to make a lot of fuss!
> End with the first verse again.
>
> ### Draw-around
>
> Towards the beginning of the ten sessions, we set up an activity in which parents or carers drew around the shape of their child's hands, taking it home to colour in. Helpers would then help children draw round their adult's hands. Later on, we had the same activity but involving whole body shapes – a more personal activity than the first.
>
> ### Shake up
>
> The adults were asked to place their child in front of them (or cuddled into a lap). When the leader shook a tambourine, they were asked to shake their child gently all over and share the fun, stopping when the tambourine was struck again. This is repeated three or four times. Later on, they had their children facing them and shared eye contact and fun as they wobbled together.

Nurture corners

Some children will be more emotionally vulnerable than others and it makes sense to plan how you will nurture them towards better resilience. *Nurture groups* were first developed in the Hackney area of London by psychologist Marjorie Boxhall as a means to help more vulnerable children. As an approach, it has been shown to reduce the number of children excluded from schools on account of their behaviour. The groups attempt to replicate a form of family life based on intense personal interest and positive support from the teacher or classroom assistant. Each child is helped to feel special and valued. There are shared meals, and an emphasis on early sensory play and familiarity (Bennathan and Boxhall, 2000).

We adapted the idea of *nurture groups* within some of our early years settings by creating dedicated nurture corners in the room with low lighting, soft surfaces, cushions, soft music, 'feelings books' to share (there are ideas at the end of Chapter 8) and cuddly toys. There was comfortable space for a key person and baby or child to settle together and we made sure that they were not disturbed by lively visitors coming in and out of their space, or by strong stimulation. Some of our less settled children opted to spend time in the nurture corner at the beginning and end of the session to assist with transition times. With older children, they chose themselves how they would like their corner to be set up, and Polly (a persona doll) was always there to assist and reassure.

Combining approaches

In practice, you are most likely to combine a variety of approaches when planning interventions for emotionally vulnerable children. Following is an example of how one setting managed to reduce Lulu's extreme crying behaviour.

Crying

Pen picture

Lulu is three and still cries frequently (despite having been in nursery for over a year), especially when her mother drops her off or collects her. Lulu's mother has found this very difficult and is clearly anxious about her. When she is occupied and busy, Lulu mixes well and seems confident in her interactions with other children. However, if things do not go her way, she tends to cry loudly and cling to a member of staff.

How staff worked out what to do

Lulu was a bit of a mystery; despite being so tearful, she could also present as a confident child and there were times when she showed that she really enjoyed her nursery. Her key person decided to start with an observation, recording when Lulu appeared to be most upset, what triggered it, how long she was distressed and what brought her out of it. First of all, it was evident that the worse time was when Lulu first arrived in the morning when she would cling to her mother and shout tearfully. At the same time, Lulu's mother looked anxious and gave her daughter a great deal of attention for this behaviour. Staff also noticed that if they distracted Lulu quickly, once her mother had left, Lulu settled happily and soon forgot to be upset. It occurred to staff members that Lulu and her mother did have some separation anxieties and they were probably fuelling each other's anxiety. If Lulu cried later in the session, she always did so 'at' an adult, as if expecting attention and help straightaway. Because she was so settled otherwise, staff began to wonder if some of Lulu's crying was a learned behaviour and if they should help her to take more initiative in sorting out her own woes.

What they did

First of all, staff members worked on Lulu's separation anxiety. They asked her mother to send her in with something interesting to show her key person to bridge the gap between arrival and settling in. They also invited Lulu's mother to peep through the window to see just how quickly she settled – this was an eye-opener to Mum and made her less anxious herself. Lulu's key person planned the first quarter of an hour carefully each session, making sure that there was something

(*Continued*)

(*Continued*)

interesting to distract Lulu until she had settled in. Incidences of loud tearfulness were handled calmly by leading her to a cushion to comfort and calm herself, then using strong praise as she quietened. She was given a small bottle to fill with her tears for Mum – and found she could not! She was then helped to sort out her problem and redirected.

Why it worked

Transfer objects – something interesting to carry in and show or a cuddly toy from home – are useful ways of helping children bridge difficult transitions in their day and separate more easily. Distraction works beautifully in helping sensitive children to settle, especially if combined with a quick cuddle and a confident approach. It might have been that Lulu's crying always led to high-level attention and enquiry from others, and that no one before had rewarded her for *not* crying. Because staff combined this with showing her how to solve her problems, Lulu actually learned new ways of coping.

Baby conversations

Drawing together what we have explored in this chapter, there is much that you can usefully do to inspire new parents (and also colleagues new to baby care). Armed with what you know, help others to tune in to the babies' first attempts at communication. It sometimes comes as a surprise to new parents and inexperienced carers that babies have their own ways of 'talking' from the earliest stages. Point out how each baby loves to hear their own carer's voice. You can do this very naturally by catching the moment when a baby is responding to the voice and pointing this out to the parent or carer, suggesting that they experiment a bit with a quieter or softer tones. Some babies are unsettled and become over-aroused with noise – point out how clever they are because they are *extra* aware of sound, and suggest that they need a quieter voice to pay attention to. Other babies are extra sensitive to sights and might need fewer distractions in order to be at their best. This kind of thinking enables you to help parents and carers tune in to *their* particular baby's strengths and challenges and tailor their responses to getting the best out of them.

Demonstrate how to place your face close to the baby's, talking and singing gently. From about four months, most babies will love to experiment with different sounds. Model how to talk and then pause, allowing time for the baby to respond with their range of noises – these can sound intriguingly like real words sometimes! By doing so yourselves, take away any of the embarrassment that a new parent or carer might feel about talking with a baby who cannot yet use words back. At all times, respond to the babies as full-blown human beings – with all the respect, greetings and farewells that you would give to each adult.

Tuning in to babies and children at early stages of development

Whilst it should be easy to tune in to children who can talk to us and tell us their views and feelings, it can be more of a challenge to tune in to very young babies or to children who have complex disabilities. One way of helping colleagues to tune in to children who have severe and complex needs and who may not be able to communicate with you clearly is to develop a 'child passport' for them. This goes far beyond the usual questions about care, diet, allergies and contacts and aims to get to the core of 'what makes me, me'. There could be pages on 'all about me', friends and family, particular interests and dislikes. For older children, open-ended questioning such as, 'Tell me about a favourite toy /activity/ family outing/ memory', 'Is there anything which makes your child particularly worried?', 'How much help does she need when going to the toilet?' or 'How does he let you know when he is cross / happy / upset?' allows the practitioner to gather honest information about all children regardless of their ability level or stage. Some settings have involved the children in designing and illustrating these to make an attractive document to share with all the new parents and carers.

It follows from all we have explored so far that one of the basic needs of the young children in your care is to be able to make their needs known clearly to you and to have these responded to with sensitivity. Before language has developed, it can be difficult for those unfamiliar with a child (such as new staff members, babysitters, other parents) to understand how the child makes his or her needs known. This difficulty becomes even greater for young children with a disability whose language skills may be delayed or for whom non-verbal communication (such as signing) is being used.

Oscar had been diagnosed with cerebral palsy and had not yet developed speech by the time he was two. His family put together a *communication book* for him. Laminated for easy handling, it consisted of a series of photographs and hung from his buggy wherever he went. Each page contained a photograph of Oscar signalling a particular feeling or need, with a corresponding sentence such as, 'In this picture, I am angry or upset. When I look like this I like to be cuddled' or 'Here I am hungry or thirsty. Please ask me if I am hungry or thirsty and I will smile and vocalize to let you know'. Each photograph had a unique combination of expressions, body language and even facial colouring (for example, the first flush of sleepiness for 'I am tired in this picture and ready for a sleep') that signifies to the adults what is going on. Through the communication book, Oscar could then communicate his needs quickly to those who were just beginning to become acquainted with him.

The question of discipline

This is a tricky question: at what age does 'discipline' become an issue, and is it helpful to see children as being wilfully 'disobedient'? We have already explored how young babies are all feelings and reaction. Discipline comes into play only once the child's higher brain has matured to the point where behaviour can be self-controlled. Up to that point, you will be potentially damaging the baby by triggering the lower brain reactions of threat and attack. With babies and most toddlers, you are working instead to provide the right stimulation for learning and development, tuning in to their feelings and needs, and providing soothing and comfort in distress.

For older children (and remember, we are discussing *only* children from 0 to 5 here), becoming antisocial or becoming withdrawn is often a learned reaction to frustrating or hurtful experiences. It might be the product of lack of emotional attuning or inconsistencies in their lives. It therefore makes sense to offer these young children support and coping strategies, as well as making sure they receive as many positive experiences as possible in their setting, rather than seeing your role one of ensuring sanctions or punishment. Meeting their needs thus involves helping them to manage their own behaviour, using positive praise and encouragement, boosting self-esteem and actually teaching those social skills which are lacking. We achieve this through clear rules and boundaries for behaviour, using simple clear language to explain the behaviour you are expecting, using choices and consequences, rewarding appropriate behaviour and remaining clear-headed, calm and consistent throughout: no mean feat! Discipline is a real challenge in early years settings, and you will learn more about it throughout the rest of the book.

References

Bennathan, M. and Boxhall, M. (2000) *Effective Intervention in Primary Schools – Nurture Groups*. Second Edition. London: David Fulton Publishers.
Bowlby, J. (1988) *A Secure Base: Clinical Implications of Attachment Theory*. London: Routledge.
Mortimer, H. (2006) *Making Connections: Promoting Attachments between Parents and Carers and Their Young Children*. Stafford: QEd Publications.
Read, V. (2014) *Developing Attachment in Early Years Settings*. Second Edition. London: Routledge.
Sunderland, M. (2007) *What Every Parent Needs to Know*. London: Dorling Kindersley.
For information on strengths-based approaches for working with individuals, visit www.iriss.org.uk/resources/strengths-based-approaches-working-individuals and http://innovativeresources.org/

2 | Personal and social development: Fitting in and making friends

As young children learn to make relationships, they need our help to navigate the complexities and subtleties of their social worlds. In Chapter 1, we explored the early stages of signalling their needs and developing the give and take of early social interactions. As children develop and begin to interact within social groups, they learn to play co-operatively, taking turns with others. They also come to take account of one another's ideas about how to organise their activity. They learn how to show sensitivity to others' needs and feelings, and to form positive relationships with adults and other children. This chapter unpacks the typical stages that children travel through in developing these skills and this understanding.

Ages and stages

If you have had experience of working or living with very young children, then you will know that there are wide differences in the ages at which they reach new milestones. Walking and talking are classic examples of this – without there being anything wrong with children, they might begin to walk at eight months or even almost two years. Some learn to crawl very early on, and others are content to lie and watch the world go by for several months, perhaps bypassing the crawling stage altogether and perfecting an efficient 'bottom shuffle'. Some are using several single words by the time they are one. Others use very few and speak 'gobbledegook' until they are two, when they suddenly produce whole phrases.

In the same way, children learn appropriate behaviour at very different stages, and this will be related to the dispositions they are born with, the way they are responded to and the experiences they meet in their world. It is constructive if you can gain an idea of the stages that children go through when they are developing social behaviour. This helps you to see their behaviour in developmental terms and not as a problem. For example, in one survey (quoted in Green, 1984, p. 21), two-thirds of parents of two-year-olds reported that their children took toys from other children or hit out at others. One hundred per cent of parents of two-year-olds reported that their child was always active and hardly ever still, and this reduced to 40% for parents of four-year-olds. Can we then say that these are problem behaviours?

Of course we can support that child in developing new ways of behaving and playing, but that should be part of our everyday early years education and care and not carry the suggestion that there is something amiss with the child. As soon as behaviour is seen as abnormal, there is the danger that the child is seen as defective in some way, and this can cast a shadow over the whole way in which behaviour is handled in the future and how that child is seen and related to. This came through to me loud and clear in just one session of my regular behaviour clinic.

> ### Thinking point: What is normal?
>
> The first family consisted of two serving soldiers who arrived in full fatigues and boots, holding the hands of a bright-eyed and cheerful 18-month-old between them. When I asked how I could help, they told me that they were worried that their son might turn into a knife-murderer 'because he heads straight for the drawer with all the knives in it and isn't interested in playing with anything else'.
>
> The second family complained that they had always had Sunday lunch at a particular golf club and could no longer go because their two-year-old behaved so atrociously. Surely it was time she learned to fit in?
>
> The third single mother was sad that her relationship with grandparents had broken down because her three-year-old was always breaking the china when they visited. Gran had suggested that he be seen for AD/HD (attention deficit hyperactivity disorder), as he clearly couldn't do as he was told.
>
> So here you have here different sets of parental emotions – anxiety, anger and sadness – all with a feeling that there was something wrong with their child. I could have said, 'There's no problem – go away and enjoy each other!' But did these parents need more than simple reassurance?
>
> What advice would you have given?
>
> What steps can early years practitioners take within their settings to spread the word about what is 'normal'?

How personal and social skills usually develop in the early years

If we are going to think about how to assess children's development in their personal, social and emotional skills, then a good starting point is to consider how these skills normally develop over the first five years. This is a wide area, and I have chosen four strands to consider: how children learn to get on with others, how they learn about 'right' and 'wrong', how they begin to speak about and understand feelings and how they develop personal independence.

Getting on with others

Friends provide each other with a sense of security and also provide standards against which one can measure oneself. Friends also act as partners for activities which cannot be engaged in alone, guides to unfamiliar places, and apprentices who confirm one's developing sense of competence and expertise. As such, the processes of peer friendship and relationships are bound to affect the development of the child's self-respect. There are developmental stages in children's concepts of friendship. In the early years, friends tend to be 'momentary' playmates; that is, whoever the child is playing with at the time. By the age of five to seven, playmates are the children seen most frequently who share things, 'act nice' or are 'fun to be with'; moreover, 'When I don't play with them, they don't like me'.

We believe that social competence emerges mainly from children's experiences in close relationships. Two kinds of relationship appear to be important to the developing child: vertical and horizontal. Vertical relationships with a carer or older nurturer provide children with protection and security during the many years which must elapse before they can make it on their own. Basic social skills emerge within them. Horizontal relationships, on the other hand, are the contexts in which children elaborate these skills with individuals similar to themselves. Horizontal relationships only begin to form usefully at the stage of three years and over in most cultures.

Early years carers are well placed to nurture the momentary playmates necessary to build up social confidence and independence. Most young children seek out and enjoy other children. If they find themselves on their own, they will tend to join an ongoing group or activity, particularly if there is an interesting adult there too. Over the first five years, there are sharp increases in the strength of children's attachment to peers generally, and social relationships, particularly within gender, become closer, more frequent and longer-lasting.

Young children are not as egocentric as previously thought, but at two are able to offer and accept toys from each other, and at three can play co-operatively and take turns. However, spontaneous sharing is rare, usually occurring only when another child requests it and this same child has shared in the past. Sharing and co-operating can enhance pupil relationships between different ethnic groupings, develop positive social relationships, and make school a more positive experience later on. Moreover, when children experience structured co-operative learning, they are less likely to develop prejudices against ethnic or gender groups. Early years children learn that teasing is an effective form of torment, but children who view themselves and others positively are more likely to take a stand against discrimination and social injustice in the long run.

Direct observations of children in their early years show that they engage mostly in solitary play, in which they pay no attention to their peers, or in parallel play, in which they play next to each other but do not interact. After the age of three, play typically becomes more associative (in which children play together but not in a co-ordinated manner) or co-operative (in which children share a goal or mutual roles).

Understanding 'right' and 'wrong'

Kohlberg (see Lickona, 1985) proposed six stages of moral development as an extension of Piaget's earlier theories of development. He saw his stages as a fixed sequence though researchers would argue that a child would be likely to demonstrate moral reasoning from more than one stage at any one age, depending upon the context and the dilemma faced. During the first phase of *heteronomous morality*, rules are accepted because of the punishment or damage which might follow. Young children see 'being good' as doing what they are told. They also see it as OK to behave like that if there is no one there to stop them or tell them off.

By the second stage of *individualism, instrumental purpose and exchange*, the developing child begins to see that, although he has his own interests, other people's interests must be served too if the world is to be fair. By the third stage of *mutual interpersonal expectations, relationships and interpersonal conformity*, children develop a need to be a good person in their own and other people's eyes; they see it as good to live up to expectations and to maintain mutual relationships, trust, loyalty, respect and gratitude. It is at a later fourth stage of *social system and conscience* that children begin to see 'right' as being that which contributes to the society or group. For the first ten years, reasoning at stages one and two predominates.

In an early years setting, we might expect children to base most of their moral judgements of right and wrong on the code of rules they have been given by their primary caregivers. In turn, we might expect that children who have been subjected to inconsistent or mood-based control to have to learn new rules once they come into the setting. New behaviours may well need to be learned from scratch, and inappropriate behaviours stopped and replaced. Some children might need to learn afresh that doing what they are told can be as fun and attention-getting as behaving inappropriately. Practitioners cannot assume that their new intake will have the same concept of being good (or not) as they do. Moral reasoning with very young children about what is right and what is wrong is usually ineffective; helping children to understand what the consequences are is likely to be much more successful in changing behaviour.

Feelings and social worlds

Between the ages of two and five, children learn to recognise and label different emotions from facial expressions and situations, usually discriminating between happy, sad and angry feelings. Increasingly, they understand that the source of an emotion can be from within as well as from without, and that emotions can endure over time or be related to memories and imaginations. Children appear to learn emotional responses through a number of routes: some seem to be present from birth and appear across differing cultures; others may be learned from parents and through experiences. Watching others can be a potent way of learning how to react, ways of expression, and what to call these feelings and can also be used to help children cope with stressful situations and events.

Early years children are able to express concern over each other's welfare and show great interest when another child is upset or hurt. Emotions are bound up with all our interactions and relationships. Learning to be aware of one's own emotions, to recognise other's feelings, and to express emotions genuinely and appropriately are important aspects of early social adjustment.

Becoming socially independent

The one-year-old will typically begin to help co-operatively when being dressed and undressed, moving on to managing simple articles of clothing without difficult fastenings within the second to third year. Shoes and socks can usually be managed by the three-year-olds, so long as laces are not involved (though we live in the age of Velcro fastenings). Most three- to four-year-olds can put on a loose jacket, though they often require help to place the zip into its foot.

Toilet-training is usually completed by two-and-a-half, though there is enormous variation in this, bowel control usually emerging just before bladder control, girls just before boys, and daytime before night-time. It becomes meaningless to talk of typical ages, since so much will depend on whether and how the skills have been taught or encouraged, whether the child is striving to be independent, and any emotional experiences bound up in the process. I have learned over the years that it can be disastrous for parents or carers to make a stand on toilet training, since the emotional factors which become bound up in the process can have long-standing negative effects on future development. As ever, the message is, 'Go with the child'.

The same can be said of feeding times which must remain relaxed and happy, preferably following a set social routine in which plenty of mess and plenty of time are allowed. As babies begin to learn to reach out and touch, their first moves towards feeding themselves will be to dabble, smear and spread their food. The first serendipitous touches of a messy hand to a mouth will herald early finger feeding and will eventually develop into attempts to transfer a ready-loaded spoon to the mouth. Then comes the stage of parallel feeding, with toddler and carer sharing the feeding process, which allows for the adult to shape the child's skills, stepping in to provide just the right level of help and encouragement to build independence.

You can see how counterproductive it is when families rush to 'get the job done' or when practitioners 'leave a child to it' before the child is ready to manage alone, stepping in to finish quickly once the trolley is about to be removed! As soon as there is an emotional dimension to feeding and toileting, the whole process of independence training is going to take you a lot longer. For older toddlers, it helps to offer a certain amount of choice and to make use of distraction (such as creating patterns with the food on the plate or flying in the spoon like an aeroplane) but do avoid 'battlegrounds' if you possibly can.

Exploration and learning

When thinking about the development of personal and social skills, it becomes impossible to separate other aspects of child development which will impinge on social behaviour and understanding. Playing socially and cooperatively also depends on a certain level of problem-solving ability. Problem solving occurs when children figure out how to use available material or resources to achieve a goal. Both experience and age appear to contribute to this ability; children who had had past experience of playing with tools and resources solve practical problems more quickly than those who do not. It is known that children who have secure parental attachments have an advantage in the confidence this attachment gives them to explore both their physical and social worlds.

Grown-ups sometimes see young children's lack of attention as a problem in their development, but attention span varies enormously, and what is 'normal' actually covers a much wider range than many believe. Concentration and attention appear to develop over four areas. First, children must learn to control their attention (such as when choosing to give attention to one thing over another), then to adapt it to a broad or narrow focus as needed (to narrow attention to one thing or to broaden attention to watch a whole series of events), then to plan their attention (for example, to ignore the television in preference to playing with toys) and finally to extend attention and concentration for longer periods. In fact, looked at in this way, 'selective deafness' becomes an advanced stage of attention development rather than a rudeness in itself!

Being bossy

Pen picture

Maya is three and loves to organize everybody. She is always first to join in activities, though her attention span is still quite short and she is quickly distracted by what is going on around her. The problem is that she will often interfere with other children, especially those younger or smaller than herself. She will try to lift them bodily towards what she wants them to play with and will not take no for an answer.

How staff worked out what to do

Staff realized that this was a rather general problem and difficult to define. So they started by discussing Maya as a team and deciding more clearly what the problem was. They decided that Maya had a difficulty in listening to others and taking on board what they said, and she also had a tendency to take over another child's play without first negotiating with that child. This made it easier for staff to keep a diary record for a fortnight in order to observe more closely how Maya was playing. They decided to record incidences where she managed well without demonstrating the problems as well as incidences where she played less successfully. They also talked to Mum, who explained that Maya was the oldest of six cousins who lived close by and never resisted her! They decided that Maya needed help to negotiate more when she played with others and to understand another's point of view. They also felt that *all* the children needed help to become assertive and to think about feelings. Finally, they thought that Maya would benefit from more work on teaching her the skills of looking, listening and holding her attention.

What they did

Staff planned a multipronged approach. They introduced a regular music *circle time* to help the children see each other as individuals, develop their confidence and assertiveness in a group and develop looking and listening skills. Maya was given specific praise for joining in so well, for looking, listening and waiting her turn in the circle. During story time, puppets were introduced and used to act out scenarios that mirrored what the staff were trying to teach Maya. Maya was also given little jobs of responsibility to do in which she could appropriately take the lead and help to organize others – handing out the snacks, helping to tidy up and showing another child how to work the computer. One member of staff was allocated to support Maya for ten minutes per session, helping her decide who she wanted to play with and then showing her how to negotiate entry to their play. This work was followed up throughout the rest of the session by stepping in and supporting Maya when she wanted to play with somebody else.

Why it worked

During circle time, each child can respond as an individual despite being part of a large group and it can be an excellent way of teaching interpersonal skills. Maya had never stopped to think about why other children might wish to object to her advances – indeed she did not stop to think about much at all as she played and flitted between activities. As she learned to extend her attention a little, she could understand what her helper was explaining to her, and she began to really enjoy putting her new skills into practice. The little jobs of responsibility made her feel valued and important. She loved the puppet play and spent happy hours teaching the puppets how to behave in a friendly way! Staff members were careful to catch Maya being friendly and use specific praise to let her know that she was doing well.

Personal and social development

Learning to communicate

Another vital developmental area that affects children's social behaviour and understanding is the stage that their communication skills have reached. Lacking the language to express your feelings and needs creates great frustration, which in turn affects how young children behave towards others. We saw in Chapter 1 how much of their interaction and responses are based on feeling and reactions, long before there is internalised language and higher brain connections with which to reason.

At the age of six weeks, most babies begin to smile as they catch the eye of their parent or carer. This reaction brings such a warm response from the adult that communication flourishes and grows quickly. For each gurgle or sigh which the baby makes, we tend to echo back in the same tones, holding eye contact and sharing the warm pleasure of the exchange. These two-way early conversations develop naturally into looking, listening and communicating and much of the flow of speaking and listening has been practised regularly even before the child develops words to speak.

Over their first five years, children gradually learn how to wait for a pause rather than to interrupt, how to share a topic of conversation so that both of you understand what is being talked about and how to begin to see another point of view as well as their own. They begin instinctively to understand what communication is appropriate and what is not (such as the three-year-old who demands loudly and publicly, 'Why is that old lady crinkly?'). These are complex and difficult skills to learn, yet most children have picked up many of the rules of social communication by the time they start formal schooling. In Chapter 7, we will explore some of the ways we can support early years children whose social and communication skills do not follow the usual path; these children are sometimes diagnosed with a condition on the autistic spectrum.

Spotting 'ta-da!' moments

Perhaps you remember the drum roll that builds up to the circus performer's trick and the final *ta-da!* of the band as the successful climax is reached. I have often fancied that I can hear that triumphant ta-da! when I spot children doing something simply amazing. We have read about development, we have understood about children's early brain development and then – suddenly – you spot one of the those moments when you can almost see children's learning and connections being made right in front of your eyes. The ta-da! factor comes not only from what you are observing with your senses but from the reflections and learning that you yourself have been through to reach this point of being able to recognise what is happening. It is a special moment not just because of how the child is behaving but because of how you are interpreting it. Spotting, and knowing how to respond to, these ta-da! moments is all part of your tool box for supporting personal and social development. Remember that this sometimes means having the confidence to stand back and not interfere when very appropriate and rather special learning is going on.

For example, Ellie needed her time to think before she was ready to share and celebrate her exciting discovery. Ellie was an eight-month-old in a busy day nursery whom I was observing as part of a 'listening to babies' project in a local authority (Mortimer, 2007). Through the luxury of being able to follow her every move throughout her long day, I was able to observe many of these ta-da! moments and, by reflecting them back to colleagues later, inspire their own insights as to the learning they were fostering (and indeed the barriers they might be putting up too). Taking time to sit back and observe behaviour (whether or not there is a 'problem') is a brilliant way to develop reflective practice and tune in to the children in your care, especially if you feel able to share findings with colleagues in a non-threatening way.

Ellie, as ever, soon began to remove as many items of clothing as she could and bottom-shuffled her way around the shallow water tray in the wet area. Soon her clothes were scattered over the entire nursery floor (and I silently thanked the staff for not busying themselves with tidying these up or insisting that she put her clothes back on). Later, Ellie came across one of her socks and looked delighted. She picked it up, studied it and tried to stick it onto her leg with repeated movements. The ta-da! moment came when she later found the second sock, gathered the two together and appeared to compare them thoughtfully. She then looked around to share her joy with the other children and adults in the room. In one almost accidental moment, Ellie was demonstrating early independence skills ('Socks go on legs!'), early mathematical understanding ('One and one, both the same, make a pair!') and early social skills ('Look at me learning successfully!'), and the learning connections made relied not just on her own serendipity but on how others shared the moment with her.

I mentioned barriers too. There was one moment in her day when the children were sat at table waiting for their mid-morning snack. Along came the carer with the cloth – disastrously swooping in from behind without so much as a 'by your leave'. The ta-da! moment came this time when the practitioner himself realised that he was actually contributing to unsettled behaviour at snack time and that he could instead approach the children from the front with all the reassurance, explanation and respect that this would involve!

Musical circle times

In the next chapter, we will look into why circle times in general seem to be so helpful in promoting children's emotional development and self image. However, musical circle times warrant a special mention in this chapter because of the way they can be used to promote personal and social development from nought to five years old. I researched this as part of a doctoral thesis at the University of Sheffield and found that, when practitioners organised a regular music circle time in their settings, this could not only be used to improve the children's looking, listening, communication and social skills (indeed their skills across all of the areas of learning), but it also improved the social confidence of many of the children and their willingness to try new activities (Mortimer, 2008). The more surprising result was that practitioners found that the children's general behaviour during the rest of the session was improved, possibly because of the new skills the children had learned but also (I suspect) through the new confidence of the adults in asserting themselves positively and effectively within a large group. We also used the approach as a useful way of planning inclusive activities for children with additional needs by devising a simple developmental checklist to observe the children and encourage next steps, as in the example below.

Music makers

Jesse was twenty months old and lived in an isolated hamlet where there were no community groups or nurseries for children under the age of two-and-a-half. His health visitor had concerns for him, and for his mother too, since Jesse had been diagnosed with a rare chromosomal condition which affected the physical development of his hands and therefore the amount of care he needed. He attended a child development centre once a week to see a team of therapists, but this was fifty miles away. The one thing which really caught his attention and made him chuckle with glee was music.

The health visitor approached the nearest school (which it was expected Jesse would eventually join) and they agreed to join a music makers project. Jesse and his mum were invited to go into the nursery class for a half-hour parent-and-child music session twice a week, and through this his mum began to meet other parents and carers and feel less isolated. The educational psychologist running the scheme ran the first four sessions, providing the nursery staff with training and resources and gradually stepping back to support them as they planned more and more of the sessions themselves.

Each session followed a standard routine which ensured familiarity and reassurance, though songs and activities within each section were varied as new items were introduced. There would be a familiar warm-up song to get everyone going, a greeting song at which all the children were greeted by name and shared a look, a smile or a wave. Then followed a simple listening game and several action rhymes. The trick came in selecting action rhymes which were developmentally spot on for the skills that Jesse's therapists were aiming for at that stage, as well as being enjoyable for all the children in the group. Towards the end of the half hour would come the chance for each child to choose a percussion instrument and play along to an accompanying CD or live instrument, perhaps combining this with movement or marching, depending on the children's stages and abilities. With a final goodbye song, the group dispersed for snack time, chatter and home.

This was Jesse's first experience of being in a social group and, after clinging close to his mum for a while, he began to become engrossed in the music and to watch the other children happily. He especially enjoyed the cymbals and, to everyone's delight, made his first attempt to bring both his hands together into midline when his mum helped him to play them. Looking back later, his mother felt that these sessions made it so much easier for Jesse to cope socially when he started nursery a year later, and had given him the confidence to accept happily what was on offer there. She also felt that the staff already had a feel for Jesse – his strengths and his needs for support – and she could therefore entrust his care to them.

Kindling bright sparks

All children are capable of being 'bright sparks' in their own individual ways. Sometimes we find ourselves working with children whose personal and social skills – indeed their whole development – seems very advanced for their years. Of course, we are there to support, care for, educate and stretch these children too. In the past, children might have been 'diagnosed' as 'being gifted' if they had a high IQ (intelligence quotient). The term 'intelligence' has been controversial, mainly because it seems to imply that gifts such as cleverness are preprogrammed and unchangeable. There is now a school of thought which claims that there are many different kinds of intelligences, all of which affect our abilities. Moreover, these are not fixed but are capable of development and expansion. Howard Gardner (1983) writes of seven areas of intelligence, and we will explore the two which relate to personal, social and emotional development.

Strengths in personal intelligences

- Is the child exceptionally good at understanding how other people behave and feel, and does the child mix very easily with others?
- Is the child very sensitive to other people's moods and intentions?
- Does the child work easily in a team?
- Does the child sensitively lead and support other younger or less-able children?
- Is the child an excellent communicator?
- Has the child passed well beyond all the early learning goals for personal, social and emotional development (making relationships)?

This child is possibly gifted in interpersonal intelligence.

- Is the child already aware of his or her own strengths and weaknesses?
- Does the child have an exceptionally strong sense of self?
- Does the child have strong values and a clear sense of morality?

(Continued)

(*Continued*)

> - Is the child self-motivated and emotionally independent?
> - Has the child developed well beyond all the early learning goals for personal, social and emotional development (self-confidence and self-awareness, and managing feelings and behaviour)?
>
> *This child is possibly gifted in intrapersonal intelligence.*

You need to recognise each of the children's particular learning styles and patterns of intelligence so that you can strengthen weaknesses and extend strengths. Even with very bright children, behaviour can become challenging if

- they find it hard to share the limelight,
- they become frustrated by the ways in which other children play with them,
- they tend to over-organise others, or
- they cannot handle failure.

There is no single way of educating gifted and talented children, and you will need to think about this flexibly. If you follow an inclusive approach in which each child's individual needs are assessed and planned for, meeting the needs of this able group will fall smoothly into your continuum of provision. Here are some ideas you can consider when encouraging appropriate behaviour in the most able children (adapted from Mortimer, 2004):

- Group more able children together for certain activities so that they can develop problem-solving, co-operation and discussion skills.
- Take time before an activity or project to help children plan ahead, set their own targets and monitor their effectiveness.
- Help parents and carers find appropriate clubs / extracurricular classes / out-of-setting activities for their children to develop particular talents or interests.
- Work in partnership with parents and carers by ensuring that their child makes balanced progress across all areas, rather than forging ahead in one.
- Think through ways of extending the more able children in each activity that you plan.
- Concentrate on bringing an element of challenge, excitement and surprise to your activities or displays – a mystery treasure chest with some clues to be made sense of, a simple experiment to try out or the chance to plan or make your own invention.
- Try to find a particular interest or special talent to celebrate, show off and develop for each child.

- Make sure that you provide the ethos in which all children feel safe to fail, to learn from their mistakes and to try again. Commend effort rather than success on its own.

Individual differences

How much is personal and social development affected by children's personalities? Over the past thirty years or so, fashion has changed on how we view temperament and personality. At one time, personality tests were widely used and fostered a belief that you could not influence a child's behaviour much; it was all in the genes. Then professionals and researchers began to see behaviour as mainly the product of the environment and pointed out that siblings brought up in very different situations developed very different patterns of behaviour. The research on early emotional attachments provided support for this idea. Nowadays, we see both genetics and environment as playing an important role, the one interacting with the other. Whilst children are influenced greatly by the way they live and the way in which they are brought up, we can also distinguish very different temperaments and individual differences between children even within the same families. Our genes appear to determine the ranges within which we behave – we may react to things placidly for example or we may become emotional very quickly – but the situation we find ourselves in determines how we will respond within that range. A paediatric colleague once told me that he could usually spot the personality of the child-to-come within the first two days of the baby's life.

So there will be times when you will meet some very determined little personalities within your setting whose behaviour can be quite a challenge to manage. There will be other children who appear almost too laid back for their own good, and miss exciting opportunities for learning because of their passivity. This does not mean that children who are individually different are problem children. You are probably already well practised in working with a range of different personalities and you need to bring on board all your people skills in order to respond flexibly to individual differences. This is at the heart of an inclusive approach which encourages all children to feel comfortable in their own skins. We will explore this further in the next chapter.

References

Gardner, H. (1983) *Frames of Mind: The Theory of Multiple Intelligences*. New York: Basic Books
Green, C. (1984) *Toddler Taming: A Parent's Guide to the First Four Years*. London: Century.
Lickona, T. (1983) *Raising Good Children* (pp. 11–15). New York: A Bantam Book.
Mortimer, H. (2008) *Music Makers: Music Circle Times to Include Everyone*. Revised Edition. Stafford: QEd Publications.
Mortimer, H. (2004) *Gifted and Talented Children in the Early Years*. Stafford: QEd Publications.
Mortimer, H. with Sure Start Stockton-on-Tees (2007) *Listening to Children in their Early Years*. Stafford: QEd Publications.

3 Emotional development: Feeling good, behaving well

In this chapter, we explore the emotional development of young children, including their self-confidence and self-awareness. This involves children becoming confident to try new activities, and developing the preferences, understanding and language which enables them to communicate why they like some activities more than others. In time and with experience, they become confident to speak in a familiar group, to share their ideas with others and to choose the resources they need for their chosen activities. They develop the confidence and the planning to say when they do or do not need help.

Exploration and play

In Chapter 1, we explored the importance of early attachments in order to feel secure and to be able to regulate your emotions. Attachment theory also has a lot to say about developing the confidence to explore and play. When babies and young children have a secure base in terms of a familiar adult who provides that security and reassurance, they begin to venture forth and explore their surroundings, secure in the knowledge that their carer is still there to offer reassurance and 'top up their emotional batteries'. Once a young child has become 'attached' to their key person in the setting (you can see how important this early 'getting to know you' time is), you can observe them beginning to play on their own, so long as they can see you there and return to you when needed. As they grow older, you see an increase in parallel play, playing alongside another child or group, watching, sometimes copying and sometimes turn-taking in their play. As a next stage, cooperative play begins to develop, though still with a reliance on you to broker disputes and help them solve social problems or face new challenges when their confidence wavers.

The importance of self-esteem

The term 'self-esteem' is usually used to mean that people have a favourable opinion of their own worth or are 'happy in their own skins'. You can identify children whose self esteem is low by observing and teaching them over a period of time. We all have 'good days' and 'bad days' but, in general children with low self esteem

- usually have a strong need for reassurance and praise from others,
- feel insecure and lack trust in their own ability to do things or to succeed,
- have problems in trying out new experiences or in learning,
- seem to expect things to go wrong for them and appear powerless to change this,
- are reluctant to express ideas or make choices for themselves,
- overreact to failure,
- find it hard to accept correction without hostility or overreaction,
- find it hard to accept praise, and
- seem not to trust others.

On the other hand, children who have high self-esteem

- usually behave more appropriately,
- are more willing to take risks when learning new things,
- appear to be more confident,
- are better motivated to try,
- make friends more easily,
- view other people positively,
- can accept correction or suggestion without giving up, and
- develop a good sense of what they are good at and what they need help at.

Low self-esteem can be influenced by the ways in which adults behave towards children. For example, permissive caring and parenting styles in which children are allowed to behave just as they wish can actually lead to lower self-esteem. Children benefit more from clear boundaries and firm but caring structure. Children also do best where parents and teachers value the child as a contributor to daily life and decisions. Finally, children do best where explanation is used to control behaviour rather than enforcement. It seems that the best balance is where parents or teachers have the ultimate say in what a child does, but that the child is offered *choices* within that boundary.

Links between self-esteem and confidence

Children need to feel confident if they are to cope with all the various challenges they will meet in their world. Confidence and learning seem to be bound together; if a child tries something and succeeds, self-esteem and confidence are raised, and they are likely to try again next time and to learn. On the other hand, if a child tries something but cannot succeed, self-esteem and confidence are lowered, and they are less likely to try again next time and to learn from it. That is why it is so important that the approaches we design for helping children's behaviour to develop and change should remain positive and should leave the children feeling good about themselves.

Try to remember that you are dealing with difficult behaviour and not difficult children. When we get to Chapter 6, we will look at behaviour management techniques. These involve planning to reduce difficult behaviours but also teaching children new and more appropriate ways to behave instead. Therefore you cannot separate behaviour management from the teaching of personal, social and emotional development.

Lack of confidence

Pen picture

Drew is three. He started at nursery a term ago but is still extremely shy. He still cries whenever his Nana drops him off and continues to sob or to cling to one of the helpers for the first half hour or so. Even then, he remains very quiet and withdrawn and never joins in at group time. He is timid of anything new and cries if demands are made on him or if the group becomes noisy.

How staff worked out what to do

Staff members were very concerned and asked the SENCO of the neighbouring school for general advice. He suggested a period of observation to begin with, trying to tease apart what was making Drew so upset. This helped staff members to hatch the hypothesis that Drew's confidence was very low. They could see that he was a shy little boy and this was not surprising because his mother and his grandmother were also quiet and shy. Staff accepted that this aspect might not change, but that they should certainly help Drew to feel more confident within the group and to play sociably with the other children. Staff members knew that confidence and feeling successful were linked together. They also knew that children who made positive attachments within the group would feel more secure and more willing to explore and to 'have a go'.

What they did

They therefore started off by allocating a key person to act as Drew's 'secure base' within the group. They suggested that he arrive a little earlier than the other children so that he could come in quietly and settle in before the livelier children arrived. His key person stayed close to him until he had settled in and began to share with him ways of playing that he found fun and successful. She used very strong praise and a gentle, closely interested approach that made him feel valued. His key person also supported his play the rest of the session, moving close to encourage when she felt it was needed or involving him in small group play. During group time, she made sure that he was sitting with her and involved him by asking him directly and then relaying his contribution to the wider group. Story times for Drew were always held in a small group in the story corner until he became more used to coping in the large group. Finally, they used a music makers circle time (page 23), again with the key person sitting beside Drew to encourage and support him.

Why it worked

The more willing children are to have a go and the more often they succeed, the more confident they become. For very shy children, or for children with separation difficulties, this can be quite a problem – they are too distressed to have a go and therefore cannot break the cycle of low confidence. Staff members made use of attachment theory to solve this problem – children who can become attached to a key person within the group can join in better and begin to feel successful learners. It did not matter that, for a while, Drew became 'a little shadow' to his key person – this was the natural next step for him in overcoming his low confidence. In time, he began to play independently with the other children.

Emotional intelligence

For many years, psychologists have debated the controversy surrounding the term 'intelligence'. Does 'intelligence' exist as a concept, or is it simply a measure of how a child performed on a certain assessment on a certain day? Can 'intelligence' be measured in a reliable way and is it a valid predictor of future achievement and ability? Is intelligence 'fixed' by genetic makeup, or does it alter with life's experiences, and by what is learned and practised? The answer, of course, is that there is a complex interplay of nature and nurture, and we explored earlier the idea that there could be many different kinds of intelligences, all of which affect our abilities. At the end of the day, intelligence of any sort is not fixed, and it might be that 'being intelligent' has as much to do with how good you are at doing intelligence tests as who you are or what has happened to you.

From these debates, the term 'emotional intelligence' began to emerge. Mayer and Salovey (1993) defined this as a type of social intelligence that involves the ability to monitor one's own and other people's emotions, to discriminate among them, and to use the information to guide one's thinking and actions. Emotional intelligence was seen as encompassing self-awareness, the ability to manage emotions, self-motivation, empathy and relationship skills. Some would argue that these 'intelligences' are no more than social skills that can be taught or learned through experience. Others have argued that they are ways to perceive and regulate emotional thought, and some of us are better endowed than others. If emotional intelligence is to be seen as a useful concept in the early years, then we need to use the concept flexibly and look at what it is we, as practitioners, can do to foster whatever it is. Suddenly, 'emotional intelligence' becomes a set of goals and aspirations that we have for the children in our care and, as such, we can use the concept practically and usefully.

> **Thinking point: Nurturing emotional intelligence in the early years**
>
> - Can the children talk about the way they feel?
> - Do the children have a number of words they can use to describe feelings?
> - Can the children recognise when other people are happy/sad/angry/scared?
> - Can the children recall past memories and the way they felt then?
> - Do all the children enjoy and feel confident in their play?
> - Can the children show friendliness and care towards each other?
> - Can the children control their anger and frustration?
> - Can the children use words and negotiations to solve disputes?
> - Can the children play cooperatively with one another?
> - If they are feeling anxious, are they reassured by a familiar adult or friend?
> - Can each child wait just a little bit before their needs are met?
> - Can each child initiate their own ideas and contribute in a familiar group?
> - Can each child occupy themselves when playing alone as well as playing with others?
> - Is each child confident enough to try something new?
> - Are the children beginning to be aware of right and wrong?
> - Do the children feel able to make mistakes and learn from them?
> - Are they able to 'take risks' in their learning, knowing that it is safe to fail?
>
> *Source*: Adapted from Mortimer (2003).

Strategies for helping children who appear to lack confidence

We have looked at the importance of self-esteem and confidence (and considered in Chapter 1 how this is related to early brain development and attachment). What can we do within the setting to inspire confidence in the children, and particularly those who might appear anxious?

Circle times

There appear to be positive benefits for all children, and particularly those experiencing emotional and behavioural difficulties, associated with working in circles. The process of 'circle time', states Ballard (1982), involves key skills required of any individual belonging to a social group; awareness (knowing who I am), mastery (knowing what I can do) and social interaction (knowing how I function in the world of others). Jenny Mosley (1993) has designed a whole-school Quality Circle Time model which encompasses regular circle times with all the children, circles for encouraging staff self-esteem and morale, and smaller therapeutic circle times for 'children beyond' (those who are beyond being able to respond to or benefit from the usual approaches).

Deep breaths

Anxious, excited, angry or nervous children can be taught a simple relaxation approach. Ask them to sit somewhere quiet and encourage them to look in your eyes and breathe at the same rate as you, as you take long and steady breaths in and out. Match your breathing to them at first, and then slow down. Make your exhalations slightly longer than your inhalations, and let your whole body relax with the exhalations. In time, children can learn to do this on their own, perhaps learning to count slowly to five as they do so.

Key person

Make sure there is a key person to act as a secure base for any child, supporting the child's play and behaviour and keeping a watchful eye on his or her emotional needs. This person should be an emotional supporter and guide, someone who spots good behaviour and commends it rather than someone who spots bad behaviour and reprimands it.

Nurture corners

We explored this idea in Chapter 1. If you have some children who are emotionally very unsettled, design and set up a nurture corner complete with soft surfaces, gentle music, picture books, sensory play, soft lighting and an available adult ready to offer positive and unconditional time. Use this for anxious, overloaded or unsettled children to withdraw to *before* problems start to arise from their behaviour.

Personal best

Some children may feel that they can never compare to others and success might feel a long way off for them, or even impossible. Expect their personal best rather than a total improvement, then none of you will be disappointed. Help children with behavioural difficulties set their own personal best targets and monitor how they feel they are doing.

Positive expectations

Some children behave totally differently in different groups because the expectations on them are different. If you expect a child to fail ('I knew we'd have tears as soon as our visitor arrived') rather than to succeed ('When our visitor comes you'll love the way she ...'), then that is what you are likely to experience.

Special responsibilities

Many children with emotional and confidence difficulties rise beautifully to responsibilities. These give the child very appropriate prestige in front of the other children.

Take two

Sometimes it can work well to give children a second chance. If a situation has gone awry because of a child's lack of confidence, try making your own clapper board for 'take two', offer support, and then re-run the scene.

Transition objects

Some children have a genuine difficulty in moving from one area to another – for example, coming from school into after-school or entering the large space. By giving them a transfer object (such as something to show a member of staff, or a cushion to sit on, a favourite activity to get on with) you can calm down these moments for them.

Visualisation

Tense children can be helped to visualise a calm and peaceful place as a means of calming themselves. Children with difficult behaviour can be helped to visualise an incident again, this time with them behaving more appropriately. You need a short period of one-to-one attention in a quiet place to use this approach effectively.

Rules, routines and boundaries

Children feel most secure and confident with clear routines and boundaries. The problem for some children with challenging behaviour is that much of the information they are given focuses on what *not* to do, and much of the attention they are given centres on not doing it. Picture timetables are very helpful for children worried about what will happen next (such as showing pictures of arriving, group time, activity, snack time, playing outside ... and *then* it's home time).

Setting the tone

Experience tells us that appropriate behaviour is most likely if children know what is expected of them. Some children may be coming to your setting with the idea that 'play' is synonymous with 'rough and tumble' or chasing each other around. They may need to be shown how to play appropriately, and helped to understand the right and wrong times for more physical behaviour. They respond best to a familiar structure with a calm and purposeful atmosphere, but it may take them a while to become familiar with your routines and to understand that play can be purposeful and intrinsically rewarding. They may need your help to understand that 'no' really does mean 'no' – not because they are being 'naughty' but because they have not yet received consistent management.

Children also respond best where there is mutual courtesy, kindness and respect, making it easier for people to work and play together. Again, this might need to be learned in the context of your setting with the adults constantly modelling courteous and kind behaviour to each other and to the children. 'Pleases' and 'thank yous' come much more easily when they are part of the daily exchange rather than when children are confronted with constant demands to 'say the magic word'. Where the children are behaving appropriately towards one another, each individual enjoys maximum freedom without threatening the freedom or enjoyment of others. This will be most likely to happen when there are observant and interested adults ensuring that each child's needs are met, and where children are encouraged and supported while they learn self-discipline.

Supporting traumatized children

We will now explore some extremes of emotional reaction and what you might do to support the child. A disaster or life-changing traumatic experience can be terrifying for anyone. How do children under five typically react, what can you do in your setting to support them, and when should you advise seeking more specialist help? Children can become traumatized for various reasons – anything which involves a long-term or extreme exposure to fear and stress. Perhaps they are refugees and have gone through a total change in their lives via an uncertain and dangerous journey. Perhaps they, or someone close to them, have been involved in a physical disaster. Some children experience trauma following major life changes (such as a sudden bereavement or violent family breakdown) or a history of abuse. Responses to stress are very individual and how a particular child reacts to a disastrous experience depends on several factors. For example, children who have been exposed to a disaster are most likely to be traumatized if they were directly exposed to the disaster, if a friend or family member has been killed or seriously injured or if the child's school, home or neighbourhood has been destroyed or severely damaged. Try to tune in to why the children are reacting in the way that they are, so you can see their behaviour as a normal reaction to an abnormal event in their lives.

Recognizing children's symptoms of stress is not easy. Young children will often cling to parents, carers and early years staff and will worry about their parents' or carers' whereabouts. Some children appear not to react at all. Others might appear withdrawn

Emotional development

and emotionally frozen. Stress reactions may include difficulties in sleeping, thinking over and over about the traumatic event or a belief that another bad event will occur to them. Some children show unusually challenging behaviour or become extremely alert and sensitive. Others might avoid similar events, such as travelling in a car. You might notice the child moving around restlessly, regressing to earlier developmental stages (such as thumb sucking or rocking), showing close or unusual attachment reactions and generally behaving as if more vulnerable than usual. All this comes just at a time when parents and carers are under acute stress themselves and may not be able to provide their usual attention and affection. Therefore more attachment, support and affection than usual is needed in the childcare setting in order to compensate.

Meet Saba

Saba is four. Her family had recently arrived in this country and there is very little English spoken at home. When she first joined the setting she appeared lost and frightened. She shied away when adults came near and froze when noisy children approached her. She would comply when she was led anywhere by an adult but otherwise appeared withdrawn. She did not speak or vocalize, and staff members were very concerned about her. Sometimes she retreated to a quiet corner and crouched down, rocking slightly and sucking her thumb.

Sam, her key person, knew very little about her history though understood that Saba's family had fled from a war zone and were moved from one refugee camp to another until brought to safety. Sam knew a little about how refugee camps operated and created a themed area in Saba's 'corner' with a sleeping mat, a shelter, some simple cookery items, a washing bucket and dressing-up clothes. Patiently, she played alongside Saba who appeared to watch closely. In time, Saba began to reenact some of her experiences in the camp, washing the clothes and preparing food. At first, she did this over and over again. In time, Saba began to integrate happily into the setting though would often retreat to her corner when she needed to, bringing her new friends to join in or playing on her own.

A process of grieving

Dealing with trauma is very similar to going through a grieving process; strong feelings can seemingly well up from nowhere and, for a while, seem beyond the child's control. In the case of young children, it can be their actual behaviour that seems out of control for a while. You can help children grieve by patiently listening and being able to tolerate their strong feelings. Children are very aware of adults' worries most of the time, but they are particularly sensitive during the period of a disaster, and they need to know that you can contain their strong emotions at this time.

Providing therapeutic support

What interventions can you plan for children who are traumatized? When the children are ready (and you will need to work closely with the families and any outside professionals involved), you can encourage them to express their fears and anxieties regarding the disaster or event through stories, drawings, small world play, art and creative play. At the most simple level, allowing children to tell their own stories of a disaster and draw their own pictures of what happened to them and how they felt about it can be of considerable assistance in both diagnosis and therapy. Books are also valuable resources; public libraries can put together lists of available books by age group, about the environment and environmental hazards, separation and loss as well as adaptation and coping. Likewise, dolls, puppets and toys can be used in play to elicit children's concerns and conflicts and to help resolve them. Group games in which physical contact (such as action rhymes and movement games) play an important part and can encourage mutual support among children and between children and their carers.

You might need continually to reassure young children that they are safe. Provide extra comfort and contact with parents or carers by discussing the child's feelings with them at the end of the session, by telephoning during the day and by providing extra physical comfort to the child. The key person, who should already have formed an attachment with the child, is ideally placed to offer this. You can plan play opportunities such as artwork or puppet play so that they remain constructive, serving as an outlet for expressing fear or anger. Share what you are doing with the family, so that you are all working at the right pace for the child.

Greet the child warmly each day. That transition from parent to key person is an important one. Often mornings are extremely stressful for these families, and a warm smile or hug as a child walks in the door can go a long way to help a child feel accepted and wanted. Spend individual time with the child every session. Even if it is just for one or two minutes at a time, get down on the child's level, make eye contact, listen and watch. Children learn to value themselves through the eyes (and words) of others. What you say (or do not say) to children at this time in their lives has tremendous impact.

Try to eliminate stressful situations from your room and routines. Do you have a balance of noisy areas and quiet areas? Have you planned the session so that there is a balance between active and quiet activities, organized projects and free play? Do you stick to routine as much as possible, so that children know what to expect each session? Do your small world play and theme corner offer chances for children to reenact events of importance to them?

Availability of toys that encourage play re-enactment of children's experiences and observations during the disaster can help children integrate these experiences. These might include fire engines, dumper trucks, rescue vehicles, ambulances, building blocks or puppets or dolls as toys that help provide ways for the child to ventilate and act out feelings about what has occurred. You might have a 'small world' just for that child kept

Emotional development

safely in a shoebox and asked for when the child needs to re-enact his or her experiences. You can keep similar 'kits' in a suitcase, including relevant props and dressing-up clothes to be asked for by the child when needed.

Recent bereavement

What can you do in your setting to support a child who has recently been bereaved? You are in a position to provide the very continuity and stability which the child needs at this time of change and loss. Do encourage the child back to your setting at the earliest opportunity, since the atmosphere of 'normality' that your setting can give will help greatly. Any bereaved child needs to be reassured that the muddling, changing and very intense feelings he or she is experiencing are normal and acceptable. Your words can help to provide meaning and explanation to some very frightening emotions. Talk to the family to find out more about family life at the moment. You can find out the words that family members have used to explain events, and it will be helpful for you to understand the cultural and religious background to this.

Perhaps you can work with the family to build up a special book of memories and photographs, which then becomes something the child can get out whenever she or he wants to talk about the loss; for example, 'I see you're looking at your photographs; shall we talk about Mummy today?' or 'I can see that you are feeling very cross today. That's OK because you've lost a very dear grandad. Let me help you tidy up, then we'll go and say "sorry" to Ahmed together'.

When to recommend more specialist help

Most responses such as running aimlessly, clinginess, regression to earlier forms of behaviour, increased sensitivity to loud noises, loss of appetite and confusion are to be expected and part of the normal reactions of a young child to an abnormal event such as a traumatic disaster or shock. The best source of support is likely to come from those of you who live and work with the child already and are their nearest and dearest. Allow a period of time for the child to work through his or her feelings in the usual way; each child is individual, and one cannot be prescriptive about how long to leave it, so you will need to work with the family to assess things. Consider referral for more specialist support if, even after this length of time,

- their uncontrollable crying cannot be comforted and they become excessively withdrawn;
- they tremble with fright or 'freeze' and this does not respond to your special attention;

- they appear to become stuck in any of the phases of grieving long after the event. You can expect 'blips' from time to time, but unchangeable sadness, anger, passivity or resistance might need further help.

Your local health visitor or family GP should be able to advise on where to seek specialist help. For example, this might involve a referral to the local Child and Adolescent Mental Health Service (CAMHS) or to a bereavement service.

> **Thinking point: Providing the best emotional climate for early learning**
>
> Drawing this together, you can see that your setting will provide the best climate for emotional learning if the following conditions are met.
>
> - Does your setting provide an ethos in which each child can feel secure, valued and respected, whatever their ethnicity, religion, gender, disability or special needs?
> - Does your setting provide clear and consistent guidelines for behaviour, and follow positive approaches for managing this?
> - Does your setting work hard to ensure that each child develops positive esteem and confidence?
> - Does each child know whom to turn to for support?

In the next chapter, we will think more about how words and language shape the ways we view behaviour in young children. We will also explore how language and words can be harnessed to teach children ways of regulating their feelings and behaviour.

References

Ballard, J. (1982) *Circlebook*. New York: Irvington.
Mayer, J.S. and Salovey, P. (1993) The intelligence of emotional intelligence. *Intelligence*, 17, 433–442.
Mortimer, H. (2003) *Emotional Literacy and Mental Health in the Early Years*. Stafford: QEd Publications.
Mosley, J. (1993) *Turn Your School Around*. Cambridge, MA: LDA.

4 The language of behaviour: Words, thoughts and metaphors

This chapter explores how children typically develop and respond to the language of feelings and behaviour and how the words we use can influence this. In learning to manage their feelings and behaviour, children begin to talk about how they and others show feelings about their own and others' behaviour and its consequences. They come to know that some behaviour is unacceptable. As they begin to spend time with other children and adults, they work and play as part of a group, and understand and follow the rules. They learn to adjust their behaviour to different situations and take changes of routine in stride. We also think about the language used by adults when working with children's behaviour and how this can be developed to plan positive change.

Sustained shared thinking

In her book *Sustained Shared Thinking in the Early Years*, Kathy Brodie (2014) explains how this way of interacting underpins almost everything we do with the children in our settings. In a similar way, supporting the development of children's behaviour is not something we tag on but should be part-and-parcel of the way practitioners interact with the children, listen actively, share dialogue and share thinking. At the heart of *sustained shared thinking* is the idea of developing children's critical thinking processes with support from more knowledgeable adults. Therefore, when thinking about behaviour, our aim is to interact in such ways as to help the children internalize their thinking about how they and others behave, and come to regulate their own feelings and behaviour. One of the ways that we can develop their shared understanding about behaviour is to consult them and listen to their views.

Listening to and consulting young children about their behaviour

Young children have a right to have their views taken into account when we plan and deliver our early years provision:

- on equal opportunities grounds, because they are part of our community;
- on educational grounds, so we can better match activity and learner; and
- on psychological grounds, because we know that active involvement in play, care and learning increases success and well-being.

If we hold to these principles, then the same must be true about consulting them about matters to do with their behaviour. How might we do this (adapted from Mortimer, 2007)?

- We can listen to young children by getting to know each of them as an individual. Children are more likely to communicate their needs, opinions and feelings to us if we have already established a relationship with them. We are also better able to interpret what they are feeling if we can recognise the patterns in their behaviour. We understand that children tell us things in many different ways – through their voices but also through the way they behave and the feelings they express.
- We can also listen to children by establishing their likes and dislikes. We can do this simply by observing children's behaviour whilst they are at play, offering choices and noting children's selections for play activities and play partners, asking the children to record what they like and dislike on camera, talking together in groups and using simple questionnaires and one-to-one conversations.
- We can listen to young children through their art, craft and music. We do this by giving them chances to draw and paint and to talk to us about how they are feeling. Children's artwork can be talked about together and used to find out about a child's interests and feelings. Sometimes when children have strong feelings or memories, they try to express these through their paintings – by talking to them about their creations, we give them a chance to talk about their feelings too.
- We can find out what is important to children by using child-held cameras. Adults can obtain a child's-eye view of nursery life by providing a camera and encouraging a child to take photographs of the playthings, relationships and activities that are important to him or her. Practitioners can then piece together a picture of children's priorities and impressions by collating evidence from the children themselves and adding the views of parents and nursery colleagues. These can be built into a book or portfolio that can serve as a record of the child's achievements for the future (such as in the 'mosaic approach' [Clark and Moss, 2001]).

- We can use stories and picture books as a means of introducing situations and encouraging talking. Early years settings often build up useful collections of stimulus books for covering a range of new situations the child might meet; going to hospital, having a new baby in the family, living with one parent. These provide natural opportunities for exploring and talking about feelings and behaviours.
- We can encourage imaginative play as a means of introducing situations and encouraging talking. Drama and imaginative play provide excellent opportunities for meeting new ways of feeling and behaving within safe contexts. In a similar way, we will use themed play to create new experiences for children – such as going into hospital – so that they have a chance to share their feelings and rehearse their behaviour in a 'safe' and familiar situation.
- By providing toys, resources and picture books that reflect a wide diversity we allow each child to participate and to express themselves. Listening to what children have to say on equality issues shows us that even the youngest children in our settings start to learn about what is different, as well as what is similar, between people. They begin to form values and responses to these differences by observing other people's behaviour and can be sensitive to how children are included or excluded. Children are more likely to feel included and to make their voices known if practitioners make sure that the teaching materials and books within the early years setting reflect a wide range of ability, ethnicity and culture.

Here is an example of how one setting found the words to tackle a familiar problem and to involve the children themselves in changing things for the better.

Ditching the dummy

Pen picture

Tinkabell Day Nursery staff decided that it was time to do something about dummies, or pacifiers. Whilst they were well used to making provision for their younger children who had dummies, they had noticed that several of the three- and four-year-olds insisted on having their dummies as soon as their parents or carers turned up, and that this was actually getting in the way of their talking and language development. The matter was flagged at a recent staff and parents' meeting, and both sides decided to take a united stance!

How staff worked out what to do

Staff and parents had recently shared a joint training event with a speech and language therapist and picked up plenty ideas for language development.

When discussing these ideas, it had emerged that many parents found it very hard to persuade their older children to give up their dummies. Staff members decided that a group approach would be helpful, especially if they shared what they were doing with parents and carers so that their work could be followed through at home. They decided to use their regular circle time as a place to discuss dummies together.

What they did

Staff members introduced the children to a large puppet, Polly, at circle time. Polly happened to have a large dummy in her mouth and sat shyly, watching the children. On Day 2, the children were curious to talk with her and the adult suggested that they tell her their names. When they asked her questions, Polly gave muffled replies, her mouth full of dummy. On Day 3, one of the children suggested that Polly take her dummy out of her mouth, and they all cheered as she became brave enough to do so! That session, the children made and decorated a wonderful tree out of a branch and glitter. The adult explained that this was a magic dummy tree and invited Polly to hang her dummy on the tree. Polly did so with the children's help. The next day it had turned into a little teddy bear! Polly was delighted. One of the children asked if it would work for him, and the adult suggested he try. As the week progressed, all the children brought in their dummies for the tree and were rewarded with teddies! Parents and carers joined in the fuss and celebration, and everyone went home delighted. That is, all except one little boy. The staff member (prebriefed by Mum) wondered if his dummy hadn't turned into a teddy because he had ten more at home? This was indeed the case, and the next day he gladly brought them all in and benefited from the largest teddy bear of all!

Why it worked

Joint training events with both parents and staff are excellent ways of developing ideas together and working in partnership. This approach would not have worked unless both sides had worked together. Children often need a context for change so that there is a purpose and a framework – the magic dummy tree and the puppet Polly served to make the children feel involved and distract them away from the potential battle ground of ditching the dummy. Narratives, stories and metaphors are powerful ways of helping children to think about behaviour and engage with change. This was such a creative and imaginative idea, delivered with confidence and panache, that it was bound to impress the children deeply.

Talking about behaviour

As we move towards thinking about 'behaviour management' in Chapter 6, we need to reflect on the words we use to talk about behaviour and the messages this can give to others. Have you noticed that some of the words we use to describe behaviours can actually become labels in themselves? A child who bites can soon become known as 'the biter'. A child who takes things without asking becomes in some eyes a 'thief' – even though that child is still negotiating the tricky path between being encouraged to take your painting home but being told off for taking home the toy car.

When you are hoping to change difficult behaviour in a child, you need first of all to learn how to describe behaviour in clear observable terms. This helps us develop an objective and professional approach without making censorious judgments. Words like 'naughty' may seem clear enough to us when we use them, but will other people understand them in the same way? You can begin to see how very important different *expectations* are – one person's 'naughty' (used because a toddler is always opening cupboards to explore them) may be very different to another's (used because a four-year-old is hitting out in order to get a favourite toy). This is why you will now read about how to develop clear and unambiguous language when talking about behaviour.

When you talk about children's behaviour, you should choose words which are observable and clear. In other words, it should be possible for the verb or action word to be seen, heard or touched. For example, 'She is being aggressive' might mean different things to different people. You could not see the moment she started and the moment she stopped. But 'She is hitting other children' can be seen and is obvious to everyone. One way of deciding whether a statement is clear is to apply the 'Guess what!' test. If someone can rush in from out of doors and say 'Guess what!' followed by a description of what they have just seen there, and if this gives you exact information about what is happening outside, then that statement was *clear*. If you really have no idea of what they are talking about, or if you see something entirely different to them in your mind's eye, then that statement was *cloudy*.

Thinking point: Clear and cloudy

Consider these *cloudy* statements about behaviour:

- Jake's Mum needs to give him much more attention.
- Gareth is always aggressive when he plays with Tariq.
- Bethany has been 'inside out' all morning.
- David thinks very carefully about what he is doing.

- Callum seems to have a persecution complex.
- Luke is hyperactive.

Compare them to these *clear* statements:

- Crystal sat still for the whole story today.
- Nicky took a toy from Carly, and Carly started to cry.
- Every time Warren passes the computer, he cries.
- Abdul pushed three children over today.

(Adapted from the Portage training materials, www.portage.org.uk.)

When you are describing children's behaviour, follow two rules:

- Talk about difficult *behaviour* and not difficult children.
- Use *clear* language which is unambiguous and non-judgemental.

That way, you will all agree on where you are starting from and what you hope to achieve after the behaviour has changed. We can agree that a particular behaviour has improved only if we have a clear consensus about what the difficult behaviour was in the first place.

Appropriate behaviour

What behaviour are you hoping to encourage in your early years setting? If you are going to speak of 'difficult' behaviours, it would be helpful to be clear about the appropriate behaviours you are hoping to encourage in the first place. It is probable that you would like children to be able to

- feel motivated and confident enough to develop to their best potential,
- respect themselves and other people,
- be able to make friends and gain affection,
- express their feelings in appropriate ways,
- 'do as they are nicely asked',
- make a useful contribution to the group, and
- develop a positive self-esteem.

Appropriate behaviour is also more likely if positive approaches are used to raise and maintain children's self-esteem. Children who are 'nagged' constantly with 'don't ...' and 'no' tend to stop listening or trying after a while, and come to see themselves as 'naughty'. I remember the three-year-old brought in to our behaviour clinic wearing a 'Little Devil' T-shirt; 'I'm the naughty one, me!' he told me cheerfully. Children whose appropriate behaviour is noticed and praised are more likely to repeat the behaviours which are attracting your admiration and to see themselves as helpful and kind; 'Good to see you sharing the bricks, Mohammed!'

Finding the words to shape behaviour

Broken record

Try not to elaborate and explain more and more each time a child does not comply with a direct request. Instead, simply repeat the same instruction over and over – this is known as the *broken record* technique. You can talk about explanations and reasons at a better time.

Consequences approach

This works especially well with older children. Rather than 'nag', you turn your words around so that the child is encouraged to think of the *consequence* of the behaviour rather than the confrontation. 'If you continue to take Jonathan's coat, then there will not be time for any outside play. If you help, we can all go out quickly'.

Count of three

Gain the child's attention, issue a clear direction and then give a slow count of one ... two ... three as you wait for the child to comply. If the child does, praise him or her warmly. If the child does not, simply help him or her through the direction yourself without further ado (for example, leading the child towards another child to apologise, or helping the child pick up the scattered toys).

Developing scripts

Some children are at a loss as to what to say in certain situations and may end up disrupting instead. Use your observations to identify these situations and help the child rehearse what to say in certain situations (for example, how to ask another child to lend something, or how to ask someone to play with them).

Indirect statements

Sometimes you can feel that your constant requests for better behaviour have begun to feel like a constant nag and that the children have stopped listening. For older children, the use of indirect statements can make a subtle change to how your requests are received. The statements usually start with 'I': for example, 'I cannot hear if you make a noise. Please talk more quietly' rather than 'Be quiet!'; or 'We cannot go out to play until these are picked up' rather than 'Pick these up right now'.

Mediation

Squabbles and arguments can soon build into feuds and long-term disputes, and you might find yourself dealing with situations that almost feel like gang warfare and extend into the wider community. Tackle only what is possible within your situation. You can use mediation and apply a problem-solving approach to bringing two children together. First talk to one child and listen to that child's version of events. Then listen to the other. Then work out a compromise and agree this with each child separately, seeking their own ideas and contributions too. Then bring the two children together, agree the way forward and follow up later. This does not usually take too long and can save you hours of having to deal with recurring situations.

Metaphors

This is a way of *externalising* a behaviour and making it easier for a child to see that something can be done *by them* about their behaviour. For example, a four-year-old who is very tense can be shown a balloon as you play together. When the balloon is full of air, it quickly loses control if you let go of it and it flies around the room. If you can let a little air out, then you can keep control of the balloon. In the same way, *deep breaths* can release your pressure and keep you in control of yourself.

In this example, one setting was faced with a tricky personal problem which needed a sensitive approach. Mr Pongo Poo provided the metaphor they needed!

Learning to use the toilet

Pen picture

Jake is four. He is dry by day but has never had the experience of emptying his bowels into the toilet. His mum says that, whenever she tries to make him, he screams and looks frightened. He can 'hold on' for days and not empty his bowels at all if she insists on using the toilet or a potty. Jake's parents have asked the staff to help them and have promised to take him to their GP if there is no progress in the next month.

(Continued)

(*Continued*)

How staff worked out what to do

Staff worked with the school nurse, who explained to staff that there had been a great deal of anxiety at home surrounding his difficulty, and this anxiety might have made the problem worse. So they decided that a light-hearted and positive approach was needed. They knew Jake to be a sensitive, imaginative little boy and decided to use this strength to engage his interest in toileting success.

What they did

The school nurse met with parents and provided a diet sheet for Jake, making the most of those healthy foods that he already enjoyed – fruit, breakfast cereals, fruit juice and brown bread. Staff met with parents to agree this approach and proceeded with parent's permission and full knowledge of the method used. Jake sat with his key person and his mother in a quiet area with a supply of paper, coloured felt-tip pens and collage material. The staff member told the story of 'Mr Pongo Poo' and invited Jake to draw him, drawing many chuckles as he did so. As he drew, he was told the story of Mr Pongo Poo, who lived in Pooland and had to get home each night to the rest of his family (which Jake duly drew). This progressed over several short sessions, with Jake taking home his artwork to share with the family (he was proudest of the gold paper specks which he told us was the 'sweetcorn'!) After a week or two, Jake was invited by his Dad to send Mr Poo home to Pooland and actually agreed to have a go using the toilet. By this time, his diet was having some effect, and the motion was easy to pass. His father had arranged an extra surprise – as Jake flushed the handle, the effect was magical – Dad had put glitter, food colouring and soap solution into the cistern!

Why it worked

This kind of therapy is based on the principle of helping children to externalize problems and therefore deal with them better. The metaphor of Mr Pongo Poo gave Jake a *context* in which to see what was going on and allowed him to move on from his entrenched situation. The approach could not have worked had not the setting worked closely with parents – neither would it have been appropriate to deal with a sensitive matter such as this without their full involvement. Medical advice was needed at some level, and you should always ask parents to arrange a visit to the GP first to check for constipation, diet and any other medical condition. The final surprise reward from Dad was the icing on the cake!

Peer praise

Commending a child who is behaving appropriately, rather than reprimanding the neighbour who is not, can be an effective way of influencing children's behaviour for the better. For example 'Well done, Daniel – that is just what I meant. Has anyone else managed yet?'

Positive feedback

Children with long-standing behaviour problems have often learned to 'switch' off from feedback because it is usually negative. Target your positive feedback directly to the child and make it specific: 'I noticed the way you shared the felt-tips, well done' or 'I can see you've really thought about this picture'.

Rules–praise–ignore

This is helpful for children who feel as if they are behaving in a certain way in order to 'wind you up'. You can build on the fact that they enjoy your attention, but do so in a way which discourages inappropriate attention. If you see children behaving in an inappropriate way, state the rule ('Please put that down'), then ignore their behaviour if it is safe to do so and give them praise and attention as soon as they conform.

Using the right language

Language needs to be clear and positive: for example, 'Polly – come down now' 'Kieran – no throwing'. You can also use it in a subtle ways to encourage better behaviour by avoiding criticism and sarcasm and including statements like 'How can I help you?'; 'What should you be doing now?'; 'I'll give you a moment to think about this'; 'No one is allowed to bite, and I won't let anyone bite you either'; or 'Let's start again'.

Warnings

Some children find it hard to switch quickly into someone else's agenda. Give a warning before a change in activity (for example, 'It will be snack time in five minutes, so finish off now'). When it is safe to do so, give a warning before a reprimand also, in order to allow children to 'save face' and change their behaviour before you step in to stop them. In this way, you are teaching them to handle their own behaviour.

'When' statements

Show your *positive expectations* by using statements such as 'When you have tidied up, it will be time to go home'. This is clearer and more assertive than statements such as 'Would you like to tidy up now?'

One of the main ways we can encourage appropriate behaviour is to plan the environment in order to make it more likely that the behaviour will happen. We will explore this in the next chapter.

References

Brodie, K. (2014) *Sustained Shared Thinking in the Early Years: Linking Theory to Practice*. London: Routledge.

Clark, A. and Moss, P. (2001) *Listening to Young Children: The Mosaic Approach*. Available from London: National Children's Bureau, www.ncb.org.uk.

Mortimer, H. with Sure Start Stockton-on-Tees (2007) *Listening to Children in their Early Years*. Stafford: QEd Publications.

5 Environmental factors: Expectations, reactions and creating the right ethos

By this point in the book, you will have understood how attachments and security affect how children behave and how behaviour in the early years should always be seen from a developmental perspective. A behaviour might appear to be a 'problem' to some, but perhaps it is simply a stage that the child is moving through. Your role becomes more of nurturing, steering and supporting rather than controlling and directing. In this chapter, we explore the environmental influences on behaviour and thereby begin to think about creating the right backdrop for encouraging appropriate behaviour. We also look at a possible format for a positive behaviour policy and how it might be implemented in your setting.

Behaving inappropriately

Of course, there will always be times when children behave inappropriately, and it helps to know what environmental influences can make this more or less likely. When do children tend to behave inappropriately? We explored in earlier chapters how attachments, early life experiences and the affect that these have on the developing brain play a crucial role. We then saw how behaviour is bound in with the developmental stage that a child has reached in their personal and social skills and also in their stage of emotional development (and ability to handle their strong feelings). We saw that children can be affected by external stress and, given the nature of their attachments, can easily pick up on the anxieties, anger and stress of their carers. Young children can tune in acutely to emotional atmosphere, long before they have the words and higher thinking skills to reason with. Inappropriate behaviour can also be triggered when they have a basic physical need for sleep or food.

Basic physical needs: Food and drink

We know that certain foods, drinks and additives can affect behaviour and being tired or hungry also affects the hormones in the body. In fact, too little or too much sugar can wreak havoc in a child's system and, unless we understand about the importance of regular healthy eating, children can end up in cycles of 'highs' and 'lows', which is only too evident in the way they behave. Chocolate and sweets eaten on an empty stomach are bad news and lead to a short-term energy boost (often seen in children as overactive behaviour) with a dramatic drop in blood sugar level half an hour or so later.

Because their brains are still immature, young children are especially reactive to certain artificial food additives which affect the hormones that normally affect alertness and level of activity. In fact, these reactions can actually lead to parents and carers suspecting ADHD, leading in some cases to further chemical intervention. In her book *What Every Parent Needs to Know*, Margot Sunderland warns us to check the contents of processed foods and try to avoid additives such as E110, E122, E127, E150, E210–219, E220–227, E249–252 and also artificial sweeteners (Sunderland, 2007).

Regular sleep routines

We have all seen children become grumpy and negative when they are tired or have not had enough sleep. But what of the children sometimes described as 'overtired' who seem past calming and settling? Sleep deprivation is associated with imbalances in the autonomic nervous system which is responsible for regulating the body's arousal system. When the balance is interrupted, the arousal system may go into overdrive, and it becomes hard to control arousal level and mood. We become more negative in our emotions and, quite often, over-aroused rather than sleepy. That is why clear, calm and regular routines for young children really are necessary. As with everything else, the amount of sleep that each child requires varies between individuals, and settings which have a 'one-routine-fits-all' approach to daytime rests can end up facing challenging times.

Thinking point: 'Reading' a baby's behaviour

George is nine months old and attends a day nursery because both of his parents work full-time. He is happily settled there, appears to enjoy his time with the other children and the carers and is making excellent progress in his development. Recently, the setting has decided to implement a fixed routine for morning rest time. After morning snack, all the babies are placed in buggies or cots in a side area and the lights are turned low. This allows the staff to tidy up and prepare for the next stage of the day.

I am observing the situation unroll. George knows only too well what is about to happen. He is given a cuddly toy to hold and his beloved 'dodie' (his comfort dummy). He looks at them both with distaste and casts them to one side. The carer patiently picks them up and returns them to him, three times, leaving him to grumble, then protest, each time. By now, George is shouting loudly, and many of the other children are also becoming unsettled. The carer realises that George's behaviour is disrupting the other babies and wheels him outside. George is taken out of his buggy and happily plays with her in the sandpit. After a while, he begins to look sleepy, and he accepts going back into his buggy and being returned to the other children for a short nap.

- This is a carer who knows George well and understands that children need clear routines. She has also read and seen TV programmes about giving children minimum attention if you want them to fall asleep. Was this the right approach in George's case?
- Was this new routine right for all? Did George need to learn to follow the same routine as all the children? And does this make him a 'behaviour problem' if he does not do so?
- At what stages did George communicate his choices to his carer? Were they appropriate choices, given his individuality and developmental stage?

Boredom

Children also have a basic need for stimulation, and the brain recognises understimulation as stress. This is all part of the brain's mechanism for ensuring that we have input, and so the arousal system is readjusted to ensure more sensory stimulation. This is why some children might rock, bang their heads or run around screaming. Young children do not have the same resources that we do as adults and so may resort to more primitive and physical ways of reacting in order to satisfy the imbalance. Again, it helps if you can 'read' and interpret this kind of behaviour so that you can increase the number of appropriate and stimulating incidents that the child's brain is receiving. Distraction works a treat, if you can spot when a child is becoming bored or mildly stressed, so that you can engage the child's need to explore and play before boredom or stress kick in.

Planning the environment

Young children behave best when they feel secure and valued and when they are aware of the routines and boundaries in your setting. The starting point for encouraging appropriate behaviour is to think about how you structure the environment so that

- there is a familiar structure which leads to an atmosphere of calm and a sense of purpose;
- each child will be happily engaged and at ease;
- children know what is expected of them;
- children know how to behave appropriately;
- each individual enjoys maximum freedom of choice without threatening the freedom or enjoyment of others in the group;
- there are adults who are observant and supportive, making sure that each child's needs are being met;
- there is an atmosphere of mutual courtesy, kindness and respect;
- the children are encouraged to develop self-discipline as well as to 'do as they are nicely asked';
- there are a few simple and meaningful rules which have been developed with children and families, rather than many rules with frequent confrontations; and
- appropriate behaviour is noticed, valued and commended by positive staff members.

Room management

If you are going to ensure that each child's needs are being met, then you all need to be sure of your roles. It can be helpful to manage staff time effectively by each of you developing different roles. For babies and toddlers, the priority is always to have a dedicated key person who knows the young child as an individual, how they make their needs and choices known and is emotionally attuned to them.

For three- to five-year-olds in larger groups, the idea of 'room management' comes into play, especially when there are several children whose behaviour needs close supervision and support. The room management roles could be rotated to provide everyone with the same experiences or volunteers/parent helpers might be used to provide extra pairs of hands for certain of the roles. For example, supposing there are four adults in a room of lively two- to three-year-olds. You might define four distinct roles for the helpers:

- the activity facilitator, who plans and organises a structured activity, engages and supports the children as they take part and stays mainly in one place for the duration of that activity
- the play facilitator, who moves around the room supporting and engaging all the children in their choice of free play and sharing and sustaining their thinking

- the nurturer, who remains in the soft cushion area and is available for comforting and for sharing story books or songs
- the care facilitator, who moves around ensuring safety, helping the children mop up spills, managing any 'accidents', etc.

Depending on your situation, these roles may need to be combined. If a child has additional support because of special educational needs, you might also have a personal support worker (PSA) who has a particular eye for the needs of the child with special educational needs (SEN), ensuring that this child can access the curriculum and is fully included. Where the child with SEN involves behavioural and emotional difficulties, this role might include putting into effect any positive behaviour programme for the child to which you might have agreed (see Chapter 6). Room management works best when it is used as the ideal structure, but when staff are also encouraged to be flexible and use their shared expertise and common sense to support each other when necessary.

Planning play spaces

If you know ahead that some children have had certain experiences or life changes which are going to make it harder than usual for them to settle, to play and to learn then you can plan your play spaces in order to work therapeutically. Think of your 'home/theme corners' and whether they truly represent the experiences of the children in the group. Always provide outlets for creative play such as artwork, small world play and music. Look for small spaces to retreat to as well as wide areas for movement and appropriate physical outlet.

Planning activities

You really can avoid many behaviour challenges by making sure that each activity or resource is at a suitable level for the children, it suits their style of learning and that the behavioural expectations which adults have are appropriate to them. Young children, like all of us, are at different stages of maturity and developing their learning styles, and you need to plan activities which suit all of the children inclusively. For example, some older children find it easiest to attend and concentrate when they are listening. Others need to look and others still need to handle and manipulate. During the early years foundation stage, the rule of thumb is to plan the activities in a multi-sensory way so that young children can listen and think, can observe and inspect and can also feel and manipulate – in other words, to plan a learning experience which is *visual, auditory* and *kinaesthetic*.

Environmental factors

This also applies to how you yourselves present the learning activities. If you are planning a structured activity, then the ideal teaching style will be to

- *show* the children what to do (modelling the activity or providing picture, real objects or concrete examples);
- *tell* the children what to do (giving clear and simple instructions, emphasising key words or providing a simple running commentary as the child plays); and
- *give* the children something to do (making the activity practical and encouraging the *process* of the learning as well as the *product*).

The activities themselves need to be child-centred (tuned in to their values and interests), allow the children an element of choice and help them feel successful in their learning and playing.

Routines

Children need to feel secure within a setting, and this will come from a regular and familiar routine. Whilst you will always wish to retain the flexibility to respond to a learning opportunity as it arises ('Quick, everyone! Come and look at the rainbow!'), you need to aim for a familiar pattern or routine which will provide the children with the security to cope with any new changes and demands within it. This will involve a regular start and finish to your session. It might also involve regular and stable staff members with whom the children can feel familiar. A named key person should have particular care and concern for a small group of children. This might allow you to have smaller group times within the larger group session and provide a secure base from which the children can operate and play. Within the smaller group, staff can provide nurturing, can help the children plan and review their day, can use a regular welcome and farewell circle time and can keep a watchful eye to make sure that each child is fully included. Children can be encouraged to make choices in their play, and conflicts can be handled with guidance and support.

Staying safe

Your particular knowledge of a child's behaviour is bound to influence how you plan for everyone's safety. Under the SEN Disability Act, you will be expected to make 'reasonable adjustments' for any child who has a significant difficulty on account of behavioural or emotional needs. On a day-to-day basis, there are many considerations which will help to keep you a step ahead of incidents which might affect safety.

- Make sure your premises are secure to keep unwanted visitors out and energetic children in.
- Make sure that physical play is supervised and safety matting is used where appropriate with large equipment.
- If a child throws objects continuously, remove dangerous items and supervise the safety of younger children.
- If major tantrums are a problem, try to set up a quiet area for a member of staff and the child to withdraw to for 'cooling off'.
- If there is a lot of kicking, consider encouraging slippers for all the children.
- Make sure you are all trained in lifting and handling techniques.
- Use safety gates on kitchen spaces or stairways and safety catches on closed cupboards.
- You will all need to have the appropriate disclosure and barring checks.
- You need to be regularly kept up-to-date with *safeguarding* and child protection procedures.
- Use risk-management approaches to provide additional supervision and support for children whose behaviour is a risk to themselves or to others.

Preparing for transitions

Some children feel very threatened by newness and change and find it hard to cope when life does not follow the usual routine. This is particularly true for children with emotional difficulties or those on the autistic spectrum, and we will learn various techniques for supporting this in Chapter 7. In general, we need to talk children through what is going to happen and when, using picture timetables, photographs, video examples and storybooks wherever practicable. This engages their frontal brains and stimulates curiosity and interest in a new experience rather than triggering a stress response.

Thinking point: Coping with visitors

Think of an impending visit by the local fire service to a group of four-year-olds. Most will be interested in fire engines and join in happily with themed activities involving stories, creative work and imaginative play. Some may be very excited indeed that a fire engine and real firefighters are coming to visit their setting. Others will not be so sure but will be carried along by the general excitement and your reassurances. On the day, some will need no encouragement whatsoever and will be 'straight in' (though you will need to prime your visitors to present what they are

(*Continued*)

(Continued)

doing in a child-friendly way). Some will need to watch through a window before they are willing to venture out with you. Others may be happy to share the photographs and follow-up activities later, perhaps being more ready to cope with official visitors when they are a little older. Others may actually have traumatic memories which make the whole visit frightening.

- Can we assume that these visits are just what all four-year-olds will find exciting?
- How can we plan them more sensitively to suit each child?

Transitions to a new setting or when starting school can also be stressful times for young children. Hopefully you will have thought about ensuring that personal information is shared about each child between settings and, in an ideal world, also arranged visits beforehand. One nursery I worked with decided to encourage the children themselves to make their own prospectus of their setting for new children joining them, focusing on what *they* felt to be important, for parents or carers to share with their children beforehand. This sent out a clear message that the children are important and that the setting belongs to them.

We involved a large puppet, Polly, in order to make the idea more realistic for the nursery children, since they then found it easy to think about all the interesting things that Polly would like to know, or ought to know, about their setting. Children took it in turns to call Polly over and show her what they were doing and used digital photographs to capture the moment. Sometimes the children wanted to take these themselves and sometimes they preferred an adult to, so that they could feature in the photographs themselves. The photographs were then shown to the children who decided on the final selection and what the words beneath them should say. Once approved by the children, the prospectus was easily assembled from the digital photographs and texts, and the result was 'Polly's First Day at Nursery'. My favourite pages were a photograph of the snake which was permanently painted on the outside playground with the caption, 'We stand on the snake 'cos it's going in time – 'cos we have to' and a photograph taken looking right down into the toilet bowl, 'We go to the toilet *here*'!

Creating the right backdrop for behavioural development

If you accept that every child is entitled to opportunities to form mutually respectful relationships with a range of other children and adults and to be safe from emotional and physical harm, then ways of creating the right ethos develop naturally. Straightaway, you can see how isolating a child, or preventing the child from learning alongside others, are not as desirable as teaching the child how to behave appropriately. If you think about the entitlements of all children, then it is clear that all children need to be supported in their learning by staff who

- work with parents and carers with trust, respecting each other's concerns, circumstances, practices and traditions;
- are respectful of differences between individual children;
- have high expectations of all children's developing capabilities, giving them opportunities to take risks, experience success and failure, and reflect on their own learning and achievements;
- value them for their religious, ethnic/racial, cultural, linguistic and sex/gender identities, and for their special needs, aptitudes and interests;
- sensitively extend the range of each child's responsibilities;
- listen, watch, take time to understand, welcome children's questioning, follow where children lead, and provide time, space and opportunities for extending children's thinking, learning, imagining and understanding; and
- treat everyone with respect and equal concern.

Changing the environment to shape the behaviour

We can make use of what we know about environmental influences of behaviour to plan general interventions for supporting behaviour when it begins to become tricky to manage. In the next chapter, we will explore how to take this a step further and write an individual behaviour plan for a particular child whose behaviour is causing concern.

Correct behaviour rather than criticise it

Provide clear information about what the children should be doing and do not become sidetracked by emotions you might be feeling yourself with judgemental comments such as, '*You* should know by now…' or 'I've told you many times…'. We often assume that children should know how to behave but forget that their brains are still immature and they are caught up in the moment. Clear rules and boundaries help children to learn what is appropriate and acceptable in their behaviour.

Ignoring silly behaviour when it is safe to do so

Providing plenty of attention to children when they are behaving appropriately usually gets good results, especially if you have already formed the kind of relationship which makes you fun and interesting to be with. Children usually crave your attention and will use inappropriate behaviour if that is the best way to get it.

Providing choices and consequences

For developing three- and four-year-olds, providing choices and consequences engages their thinking brain rather than triggering their fear and rage lower-brain responses. They are driven to greater independence yet not ready to cope with all that this involves. You can provide choices (such as, 'Would you like me to help you tidy up the animals or will you be tidying the bricks today?'), and you can spell out consequences ('If you snatch the train, Harry won't want to play with you' or 'When you have tidied up it will be time to play outside'). These can be done at the same time as remaining in control of 'what's on the menu' and therefore allowing the children more autonomy within a secure framework.

Motivators

Children are more likely to behave if they are motivated in their play.

- Make the activity itself intrinsically motivating – appeal to any appropriate areas of interests (e.g., dinosaurs, sport) when selecting topics, themes and tasks. Sometimes children need individually planned activities at first in order to work with their areas of interest and get them going.
- Make it more motivating to behave appropriately by selectively targeting and praising positive behaviour. In order to do this, you need to tune yourself into noticing when children with behaviour difficulties behave even 'normally', let alone especially well.
- You can add extra motivators which can be used as tokens for good behaviour – stickers, smiley-face stamps, taking the class hamster home, doings special job of responsibility, a dip into a 'lucky box', etc.

Separate the 'pack'

Certain behaviour becomes ten times worse when the children are playing in a 'pack' – this is a primitive form of behaviour and predictable in social groups. Separating certain packs or rearranging the mix of children in an activity can alter their behaviour significantly, as can planning quieter and more-structured outdoor playground areas.

Shaping

When you are moving towards a particularly desirable behaviour for a child (such as being able to share), you cannot expect to get there straightaway. Start by accepting even a tiny approximation of that desired behaviour (for example, letting another child have the glitter stick for a brief moment) and praising it. This is called *shaping*, and many behaviours and learning targets lend themselves to this kind of approach.

Timeout

This is difficult in a busy group. The idea is to have a cooling down area away from an audience where a child can calm down to the point that you can then discuss the child's behaviour and agree on a way forward. The purpose is not to punish so much as to cool down. I hope that you are, by now, as horrified as I was when one setting proudly announced to me that they 'dealt with bad behaviour' by placing a large hula hoop in the centre of the room and sending miscreant children to stand in the 'circle of sin'! Children should always be supervised and safe during timeout, and it should not be used to make an example of the child to others; most services and groups will have clear guidelines on the use of this approach which you should follow. Take care that an older child sent out to the manager's office does not end up having a rather exciting time there! Often, 'time in' is more effective than 'time out' if you can play quietly with the child and talk through what has happened and how it could have gone differently.

Traffic lights

This is a helpful approach for keeping the lid on a whole group of four-year-olds. Have a set of traffic lights (invent you own system) and flash up amber as a warning to quieten down and red as a sign to stop. When everyone has quietened down, redirect them again with green. Another use of this approach is when older children are given red, amber and green cards and display them to you in a directed activity to let you know if you are going too fast for them to follow.

Running off

Pen picture

Amalie is three and loves to move at a great speed. Her mother finds it hard bringing her to nursery in the morning, as she refuses to hold hands and runs off ahead. Mum is very worried about her safety. Amalie seems to have no awareness of danger or boundaries. At nursery, she will make a beeline for any open door and will try to run off if staff members are not vigilant. Mum has asked the nursery staff to help her overcome this problem and is keen to work with them. However, she doesn't know where to start.

(Continued)

(*Continued*)

How staff worked out what to do

Amalie's key person walked home with Amalie and her mum one day just to see how bad the problem was. It was clear that Amalie did not listen to her mother and that the worry about running off was just part of the problem – Amalie's behaviour was disorganized, and she still had not learned to link cause with effect. They felt that they should first do some work on helping Amalie to listen to and follow through instructions. The manager was concerned about safety aspects and carried out a risk assessment of the security system in the building.

What they did

The manager made sure that security locks and procedures were all in place and that, at all times, there were at least two sets of closed doors between Amalie and her freedom. Notes were put up for parents and carers to make sure that doors were always closed on arrival and departure. A key person then began to play alongside Amalie, extending her play and concentration and helping her to play more constructively and imaginatively. Amalie loved these sessions and began to watch out for her key person and become more fully involved in their play together. The key person began to focus her listening skills, using her name and eye contact to tune her in and making sure she understood what was being said.

After a week or two, the key person had another walk home with Amalie and her mother. This time, the key person explained the rules to Amalie: 'If you do as you're told, you can walk without holding hands. If you do not, you will have to hold hands. When we are near the main road, you must always hold hands'. She showed Amalie which parts of the walk home needed hands and which did not. Where it was safe, she set Amalie little challenges to see if she could listen – 'Run to *that* tree, then wait … GOOD GIRL!' This kept Amalie focused and occupied for much of the journey. One more walk was shared – this time with Mum setting the rules and challenges and the key person praising her. The occasional 'top up' of help from this staff member was offered if needed.

Why it worked

Amalie turned out to be a real 'do-er' (rather than a 'looker' or a 'listener') and clearly needed much support and encouragement of her attention skills. Once she had begun to anticipate and to imagine in her play, it became a lot easier to focus her. At that point, the work on her running away had a chance of being more effective. Working in partnership with Mum and sharing progress in front of Amalie gave added weight to the approach and allowed Amalie to see that they were all working together. Mum felt better supported and more confident because of this. The staff members offered 'top up' if needed – this meant that they were determined to see the approach through to its successful conclusion.

A positive behaviour policy

If you are going to support behavioural development effectively in your setting, you need to have a clear policy which describes your philosophy about children's behaviour, how you will set about promoting appropriate behaviour in your setting and how you will manage inappropriate behaviour. You do not have to start from scratch – there are clear government guidelines which set out the standards all registered settings should aim to meet. Each registered setting should have a behaviour policy which shows how your group promotes good behaviour using positive approaches. This should be a workable and accessible document that draws together all the things that you do in your setting that encourage good behaviour in the children.

Start with your philosophy and your aims

It makes common sense for your behaviour policy to flow out of your other policies, and in particular the policies you have on SEN and on equal opportunities. Usually the same factors that promote inclusion, confidence and a sense of belonging or inclusion also promote good behaviour. Here are some of those factors which you might be able to include in your behaviour policy when describing your philosophy. Perhaps you believe in (adapted from Mortimer, 2006)

- encouraging all the children to feel enthusiastic in their learning;
- making sure that all children and adults feel included in the setting;
- finding ways of showing that you value each and every child;
- supporting children as they arrive, depart and go between activities;
- developing each child's sense of worth and confidence;
- making sure that adults feel confident and develop skills for handling difficult behaviour;
- making the transfer between settings or into school go smoothly;
- finding ways in which each child can learn successfully;
- teaching children to work and play within groups;
- showing children how to listen to and communicate with each other;
- building up children's concentration and teaching looking and listening skills;
- providing positive role models, especially through the adults' own behaviour;
- making sharing enjoyable and successful;
- findings ways of motivating each child;
- providing nurturing and comfort where needed;
- working in partnership with parents and carers; and
- using approaches that have been shown to support self-esteem such as circle time.

Describe how you will do this

The policy would then give details of how you would achieve those aims.

- You might wish to say that you recognise and support the principles of the various codes and standards which are current and list those which apply to you.
- You might wish to comment on your learning environment. You could talk about how you provide a stimulating, calm and inclusive setting and how the staff have positive attitudes, always trying to remove any barriers to learning.
- You could mention how you use your resources both within the setting and beyond to help the children become active and valued members of their community.
- You could mention how you ensure that staff are kept up to date with information and approaches to help them promote appropriate behaviour and manage any difficult behaviour effectively.
- You would mention how you work towards keeping the behaviour policy up-to-date and how you are always aiming to improve the service you provide for encouraging positive behaviour in your setting.

How to implement the policy

Your policy should then describe how you are going to carry out the behaviour policy in your setting. You might wish to include these points:

- how it is ensured that all staff understand and implement the behaviour policy
- how staff respond to children who have emotional or behaviour difficulties
- any particular roles and responsibilities of staff members
- which person has special responsibility and knowledge of behaviour management issues (usually this is the SENCO or the manager)
- a list of any special training in behaviour management that the staff had received and how you plan and monitor their training needs
- how you worked with parents and carers to design, implement and review the policy

Poppyfield Nursery School: Our behaviour policy

Our aim:

- We aim to provide a setting where each and every child feels accepted and valued.

- We want each child to feel happy and to grow in confidence, whatever their needs.
- We want all the children to develop friendly and helpful behaviour.

How we do this:

- We try to make each play and learning experience enjoyable and to make sure that each child can succeed.
- We use positive praise and show the children that we value what they are doing using praise, photographs and displays.
- We warn children before an activity is going to change.
- We *show* them how to behave as well as *tell* them.
- We sometimes work in small groups so that we can teach the children to join in and to share.
- We use a daily circle time to teach the children personal and social skills.
- The children help us to agree just a few clear rules which we encourage the children to follow with helpful reminders.
- If we need to tell a child to behave more appropriately, we do this away from an audience whenever possible.

How we respond to children who have emotional or behaviour difficulties:

- If a child does not respond to our usual approaches, we talk with the group's special educational needs co-ordinator, whose name is Ella S.
- She discusses the child's behaviour with parents or carers, helps us assess what the difficulties are and helps us plan our approaches.
- We design an individual behaviour plan to suit the child, based on positive approaches.
- We can call on the advice of the local Behaviour Support Teacher if needed, and always discuss this with parents or carers first.

How we involve parents and carers:

- We believe that the best approaches will come if we can use the expertise of both home and setting.
- We always value what parents and carers have to tell us about their child's behaviour and can use this information to plan our approaches.

(*Continued*)

(*Continued*)

> - If a child's behaviour needs an individual approach, we will discuss and share the plan with parents and carers and review it regularly with them.
>
> These staff have had training in behaviour management and emotional difficulties: Ella S., Zach N., Sue B.
>
> We review this behaviour policy each September at the annual management meeting and consult with the parents' group.

In the next chapter, we will unpack how you might plan for children who have longer term needs associated with their emotional, behavioural or social development. When preparing your behaviour policy, you will have covered the facts that plan for any children who have such additional needs – but what might this actually look like in practice?

Reference

Mortimer, H. (2006) *Behaviour Management in the Early Years*. Stafford: QEd Publications.

6 | When behaviour needs to change: Observations and planning interventions

We explored in Chapter 1 how babies and toddlers behave in the way that they do in order to communicate and to signal their needs; therefore it is up to us to tune in and to interpret their behaviours. As such, we cannot see such behaviour as a problem. We also explored early brain development and how it affects learning and behaviour.

But what of older children – say, the two-year-old and beyond – who need extra support to understand their social world and how they should interact and behave within it? You should already have developed practices for encouraging children's appropriate behaviour in your setting, and these should be along the lines of your behaviour policy which we looked at in the previous chapter. These practices will work for most children most of the time. However, there will be times when you feel that your usual approaches are not working and that an inappropriate behaviour has become somewhat stuck or extreme. In this chapter, you will think about how you can decide when a behaviour becomes a problem and what to do next.

'Problem' behaviour

If you have a child in your setting whose behaviour is causing concern, ask yourselves the follwing questions before you decide on whether there really is a 'problem':

- Is the child old enough yet for you to be considering approaches to modify and change their behaviour? Knowing what you do about attachments and early brain development, is the child too young for you to be seeing a behaviour as a problem?
- Has the child had time to settle into your group or setting? Some children take longer than others to settle into new routines, so the behaviour might settle once the child is used to your setting, your rules and your routines.
- Has anyone talked with parents or carers yet? They usually know their child inside out and can contribute useful information and ideas. What they say might allay your fears

or at least help you to understand what is going on. Perhaps there are changes at home which will inevitably leave the child unsettled for a while. What they say might also lead you to feel that you need to use more special approaches or advice. You always need to be vigilant for any safeguarding issues and follow your usual procedures.

- Have you considered that poor self-esteem and confidence might be at the root of things? If so, use a key person to befriend and support the child, using positive encouragement and support to enable the child to feel more confident and tuned in to you all.
- Has the child not yet learned to play calmly and socially? This might not be a behaviour problem but more a case of teaching the child another way to play and behave. Look for strategies to make play extra fun, and rules clear. Play alongside the child with one or two other children, showing that playing socially can be safe and enjoyable.
- Is the child not yet at a developmental stage where he or she has learned sharing, turn-taking and asking for things? It might be that the 'behaviour problem' is related to the fact that the child is still at a young stage of development.

Individual behaviour plans

You can find out more about the problem by troubleshooting and finding out which approaches help you begin to see an improvement. Identifying a behaviour problem and planning an intervention should be inextricably bound together so that knowledge of the one informs the other. You will find ideas for planning a range of interventions later in this chapter. Start by choosing a few clear rules which the children have contributed to. Talk about them during circle time. Look for opportunities to praise children specifically ('Thank you, Freddie, for giving that car to Jazz') for following the rules. Help children who do not by *showing* them what to do instead and then praising it.

If a child has had time to settle with you, and still is not responding to your usual encouragement and boundary setting, despite all these approaches, then you might consider talking to parents about using interventions which are additional or different to the usual. Consider putting together a within-setting individual behaviour plan. Below is a simple example, and the actions taken will make sense to you once you have read on.

Individual behaviour plan

Name: Daniel
Nature of difficulty: Daniel has a very short attention span and finds it hard to play socially with other children without physically hurting them.

When behaviour needs to change

Action

1. Seeking further information

Greta will be Daniel's key person. She will talk with Mum and find out which other services are involved. If there are other professionals working with Daniel's family, she will enquire about their approaches with Daniel, so that we can follow through any effective strategies in the setting.

2. Seeking training

We would like to learn more about helping Daniel handle his tempers, develop more appropriate ways of interacting with other children, and play for longer, preferably with other children. James, our SENCO, will contact the local behaviour support service for information about any suitable training courses.

3. Assessing Daniel

We need a system of monitoring and recording Daniel's play and behaviour which fits in with our nursery activities. Greta will spend the first two sessions running a STAR analysis of his behaviour (see STAR chart Section, below). She will observe him as he plays, keeping running notes of all he does using clear, objective words. Afterwards, we should have a record of both Daniel's strengths and weaknesses which we can use to settle his behaviour and develop his skills.

4. Managing his behaviour

Daniel will be given a high level of adult attention, which he seems to crave, but this will be when he is behaving appropriately. If he is looking cross and stressed, Greta will invite him to sit quietly in the cushion corner with the music tapes, so that he feels calmer. Daniel should be allowed to go there if he feels the need.

Whenever there are opportunities, Daniel should be shown how to play for longer, to share, to take turns and to share fun with other children appropriately.

Whenever he moves to hit, kick or bite another child, Greta will draw him away with a clear hand signal and saying, 'No biting, Daniel' and then sit with him quietly on the cushions for a minute. She should then talk to Daniel about what he could have done differently, and help him to apologise or restore any damage. She will support him for a few minutes as he begins to play again.

We will use circle time for choosing activities to boost Daniel's self-esteem and confidence within the group.

5. Help from parent

Daniel's mum, Jean, agrees to make a point of talking with Daniel's key person, Greta, every Friday after preschool. They will share the good news as well as the difficulties.

(*Continued*)

(*Continued*)

Targets for this term

1. Daniel will play peaceably on the train mat for ten minutes, with other children playing alongside him in parallel.
2. Daniel will play co-operatively with one other child for five minutes with Greta helping.
3. Daniel will manage three sessions in a row without moving to hit, kick or bite another child.
4. Daniel will begin to look pleased when he is praised.

Review meeting with parents: In six weeks' time. Invite any other professional who is involved.

Observation and assessment

The first step with a behaviour difficulty is to gather information through talking with the family (there are ideas for doing so in Chapter 8) and to any other professional involved, and also to spend time observing the behaviour itself. Not only does this provide you with useful information, but also it gives you thinking time to work out what you can do about it. Once a problem has been identified, everyone will be looking towards you to 'do something'. When you gather information, you are clearly doing something even though you do not yet have a plan of action formulated. Sometimes the very act of standing back a little and observing what is going on gives you the emotional distance to think about the problem more objectively. There are various ways in which you can observe and record problem behaviour. When this is done prior to a behavioural intervention it is called *collecting baseline information*.

STAR chart

Keep a diary recording what the child was actually doing, what seemed to lead up to it and what the consequences were. Write clearly and objectively, describing observable actions and using non-judgemental language. This is called a STAR chart because it records the following:

- **S**etting (what happened before the behaviour took place, the context, the situation at the time)
- **T**rigger (what seemed to set the behaviour off)
- **A**ction (exactly what the child did)
- **R**esponse (what happened as a result of the behaviour or what those around the child did next).

It is helpful if you can have 'good news' and 'bad news' STAR sheets so that you can gather information about activities and sessions that went really successfully as well as those that went badly – in this way you come to see what interventions actually work already.

Counting or measuring the behaviour

Sometimes a behaviour is so evident that you can actually count the number of times it happens during a session. This is only possible if you have all agreed together what constitutes the problem behaviour and when you will count it as happening. What one staff member sees as a temper tantrum, another could see as only a grumble – in other words, two people can observe the same child doing the same behaviour and describe or interpret it in very different ways. Behaviours which might lend themselves to a frequency count include throwing toys, upsetting toy boxes, kicking, climbing onto the tables. Other behaviours can be measured in terms of their duration – perhaps a child screamed for ten minutes today or played happily for twenty minutes continuously.

The whole point of measuring the behaviour in some way is (1) to enable you to see change, and (2) to enable you to monitor the intervention you have planned.

Unless you have recorded that you started with six major temper tantrums each session and that you are now (three weeks later) down to three, you would never appreciate the success that you are having. Instead, you would have become so focused on these temper tantrums that you would be wondering why, after all your hard work, they were still very much in evidence. Only by seeing that you have in fact reduced them by half can you check that you are probably on the right lines.

Spot observations

With older children, we sometimes use spot observations to see whether a child is 'off task' or 'on task'. This becomes meaningless in early years because *all* play is on task, and learning and play should be synonymous. However, there are occasions when this can be a very helpful approach, depending on the behaviour being observed. For example, suppose that you are worried about a child whose behaviour is very solitary. Each five minutes you could observe the child briefly and record whether they were playing on their own or with others. This would give you a baseline against which you could measure positive change. Perhaps your baseline observations showed that the child was playing on his own for 10/12 observations. After you have worked on encouraging more group and social play, you might be able to record a 'post baseline' of only 3/12. The whole observation need only take one hour of spot checks every five minutes. Repeat it in different situations and on different sessions so that you are sure you have a meaningful sample.

'Fly on the wall' observation

If you have the opportunity, observe a child over a continuous period of time (say, 30 minutes) and write down what they are doing and how they are interacting in clear, unambiguous terms. Record the time in the left hand margin so that you will have an idea of how long the child was playing in a certain area or demonstrating a certain behaviour. Where possible, arrange for extra help so that you can be released for this length of time. Ask other staff to carry on as if you were not present and not to rely on you at this time to manage any incidents or help the children. Sit somewhere to the side of the room and move discretely from area to area in order to keep the child in view. It soon becomes possible to develop the knack of observing from the corner of one's eye and recording as you watch. If other children approach, keep your eyes down and explain briefly but politely, 'I'm doing my writing today. You will need to ask ____ instead'. Later, you can look through the observation together with colleagues and identify any patterns to the behaviour. If you are a childminder, try to keep running notes as you both play with and observe the child at play – this is called a *participant observation*.

Meet Jethro

Jethro was referred to me because he was 'always creating trouble' and looking for opportunities to fight other children. There was very little positive about him said by anyone. I observed him in the nursery using a 'fly on the wall' written commentary, keeping a note of the time in the margin. He was playing with the construction toys, all by himself at one end of the room. All staff members were at the other end of the room organising an activity with most of the children. Jethro played for a full twenty minutes, creating the most fantastic model using every single item in the kit. As he sat back to admire his creation, two children approached. The first tripped over his model by accident. Jethro let this pass by without reaction. The second child (probably knowing Jethro to be likely to react) paused, gained eye contact with Jethro and deliberately kicked the model. Jethro attacked him and all the staff members came running. *'You see what we mean?'* they said to me.

- List two big positives about Jethro!
- What advice would you give the staff members?
- What would be a good target to work on with Jethro, and how could staff members support this?

Behaviour management

Behaviour management is just one of the many tools that you can use in order to change difficult behaviour. You would feel uncomfortable basing your entire early years teaching around the premise that children only behave in a certain way in order to gain rewards. However, there is a definite place for it when a particular child is displaying very difficult and demanding behaviour which has not responded to your usual approaches. It gives you a definite job to do at a time when you might be feeling disempowered or unconfident because of a child's behaviour.

Behaviour management is based on the theory of behavioural psychology and makes use of positive encouragement and reward. In essence, a behavioural theory states:

- If you do something, and something *pleasant* happens to you, you are more likely to do that thing again.
- If you do something, and something *unpleasant* happens to you, you are less likely to do that thing again.

So far, this should make sense to everyone. Suppose, for example, that you move to a new job and pluck up courage on the first day to say hello to a new colleague in the corridor. If that person smiles and say hello back, then you are likely to continue with a regular greeting and perhaps get to know each other better over time. However, if the person looks away and does not reply, then you are likely to feel less confident and not so likely to say hello the next time you meet. In other words, what happens to you in a social situation affects what you are likely to do in the future.

What of the child whose behaviour becomes *worse* after a 'good telling-off'? Should it not follow that when something unpleasant happens (like the telling-off) the child should be likely to behave *better*? In reality you know that this does not always follow! For some children, behaviour is directed at attracting *any* kind of reaction or attention, even if it comes in the form of a good telling-off. When you look back to Chapter 1 and to different patterns of attachment, you can understand why this is so. In other words, you cannot decide that the telling-off is a punishment for the child unless it actually reduces the behaviour. Each child and each situation will be different.

Therefore it is helpful to understand that rewards are not rewards because of *what they are* (eye contact and a cuddle, public applause, a special food treat) but because of *what they do* (they make the behaviour *more* likely to happen in the future). Similarly, negative consequences are not so because of what they *are* (a reprimand, a telling-off, being sent to another room) but because of what they *do* (make the behaviour less likely to happen in the future):

- The *pleasant* event is called a *reward*, simply because it makes the behaviour *increase*.
- The *unpleasant* event is called a negative consequence simply because it makes the behaviour *decrease*. We use the expressions 'negative consequences' or 'sanctions' instead of 'punishment', because there are fewer overtones of physical or negative action.

When working with young children, negative consequences need not be something unpleasant that happens; they can simply be that the child was expecting a certain reward to happen and it never did (e.g., the temper tantrum did not bring the expected tractor ride, or the bite did not lead to being able to play with the train).

Staying positive

It sometimes comes as a surprise that we should be using *positive* approaches to dealing with what might appear to be very *negative* behaviours. Positive behavioural approaches do these things:

- They make sure that the child's self-esteem remains positive. This is because the child is given the message that it is the *behaviour* which is unacceptable rather than the child.
- They are based on the use or removal of rewards and pleasant happenings. Negative consequences may work in the short term to control or stop a difficult behaviour, but they will not help the child to change behaviour in the longer term. Instead, they lead to children behaving inappropriately until an adult intervenes, rather than learning self-control.
- They aim not only to remove or alter an inappropriate behaviour but also to replace it with a more positive and appropriate behaviour. Since you are all in the business of teaching and encouraging personal, social and emotional development, this makes obvious sense. You know that children do not arrive in your setting with appropriate behaviour ready-packaged – behaviour and social skills need to be learned and developed, just like everything else.

Using rewards effectively

When you think about it, rewards are happening all the time in your setting. Adults and other children smile, give each other eye contact, make approving comments and give encouragement. All these are done quite naturally and provide motivation for the child to behave in that way again. Day by day, children receive the message that kindness, creativity, happy and constructive play and friendly conversation are all behaviours which are regularly rewarded and valued by the people around them. There are several different categories of rewards which most children will already be used to in their daily lives:

- Social praise: smiles, eye contact, a cuddle, praise, laughter, clapping hands, cheering
- Food and drink: favourite snacks, drinks, fruit, meals

When behaviour needs to change

- Toys and playthings: being able to play with the digger or the group's teddy, enjoying a new set of toys
- Activities: going to play outside, having the slide out, enjoying a story, playing on the computer
- Sights and sounds: a musical CD, a kaleidoscope, coloured lights
- Physical: a cuddle, a swing, a brush of the hair, a gentle blowing of a fan

If you see that rewards are a fact of daily life then you will feel more comfortable about using rewards in order to change particularly challenging behaviour.

If a reward is going to be effective it has to satisfy these conditions:

- It must happen immediately. It is no good saying, 'You can have a treat next week' – young children need your praise and recognition straightaway.
- It must be something which catches the child's attention. It is no good saying, 'That's wonderful, Ruben' in a quiet deadpan voice that Ruben will not even notice. Sometimes (with some children for whom praise has not been given regularly) you have to be extreme in your expression – 'That's FANTASTIC, Ruben!'
- It has to work for the child. Some children (perhaps because they have social or autistic spectrum difficulties) genuinely find eye contact and strong praise difficult to handle. It might even cause them to behave in a way to avoid it. In other words, one child's reward might be another child's sanction.
- It has to be given consistently at first. When you are introducing behavioural approaches, you need to realise that you should reward or praise every single time a child behaves in the targeted way at first. Later, as the new behaviour becomes established, rewards can be given every now and again and gradually phased out.
- If a concrete reward (such as food or a toy) is given, perhaps because that is the only thing a child will work for at first, then social praise should always be given as well. In time, the concrete reward can be faded out as the social praise remains. In time, the child will come to find the social praise alone to be rewarding. When the child is older, the aim is for him or her to be behaving in the appropriate way through self control and self discipline.
- You can use your own knowledge and experience of the child in order to work out which rewards will be effective. Parents and carers will also be a useful source of information. Perhaps their child collects certain stickers at home or loves a certain play activity. Perhaps the child is on his or her very best behaviour when looking after the family pet. Perhaps the child loves yoghurt snacks. Perhaps the child loves to be the family clown and to be cheered and applauded. Remember that each child is unique.

Planning changes

The best way to change children's behaviour is to change what you as an adult are doing. Below are seven easy steps to help you design a simple behaviour management programme in order to change a particularly difficult behaviour (adapted from Mortimer, 2006):

Step 1: Describe the behaviour(s) you are concerned about.

Use clear language and reach concurrence with colleagues and parents so that you are all clear about the behaviour which you wish to work on.

Step 2: Observe the behaviour.

If you are going to change a difficult behaviour into a more appropriate one, you need to know where you started from and when you have 'gotten there'. Your starting point is called the baseline. It gives you a clear picture of how difficult or frequent the behaviour was before you started your plan to change things. You can measure behaviour in the different ways suggested earlier in the chapter. You should end up with a clearer picture of the settings, the triggers, the actions and the responses.

Step 3: Gather information.

It is helpful to find out more about the child's behaviour in different situations. Speaking with parents or carers is the obvious starting point. Behaviour can sometimes be a sensitive area to discuss with families without arousing defensive feelings. There are more ideas about this in Chapter 8. There might also be useful information to be gleaned from any other professionals involved such as a health visitor, family support worker, community worker, social worker or child psychologist. Perhaps the child used to attend another group; what was the behaviour like then and what approaches helped?

Step 4: Select just one behaviour to work on first.

When you gather information about a child's behaviour, you might end up with a whole list of difficult behaviours and situations. You can feel daunted unless you understand that the best place to start is on *just one behaviour* – perhaps one that is easy to change (such as running into the kitchen area) or one which is causing most disruption (such as biting). You can reassure everyone that this approach can help other behaviours too by starting a positive spiral of better behaviour, more positive self esteem and a happier child.

Step 5: Decide on a hypothesis

What do you all think is keeping that behaviour going? Is the child behaving like this to seek attention? Is it because the child cannot yet play co-operatively? Is it because the child has not yet learned to share? Is it when Mum brings the child to the group and not

Gran? Try to become a behaviour detective and, armed with all we have covered in this book, hatch your best hypothesis as to why a child might be behaving in this way.

Step 6: Draw up a plan to change the setting, the trigger, the action or the responses (see below)

Step 7: Monitor progress over three weeks and then review.

Review your hypothesis and your interventions if you need to. Behavioural approaches take a little while to work. If, for example, you have drawn up a plan to reduce attention-seeking behaviour by reducing the amount of eye contact and reaction you are giving the child, the behaviour is likely to become worse before it becomes better, since the child will be testing the boundaries for a while.

Changing the setting and trigger

What are the most common approaches you can follow for changing the setting (or context) of a difficult behaviour? Many of the approaches in this chapter have been adapted from the Portage teaching approach. Portage is a home-visiting educational service for pre-school children with additional support needs and their families, and training in behaviour management is part of their three-day basic training workshop (visit www.portage.org.uk for further information).

Avoid likely situations

You may have begun to see a pattern emerging. Perhaps the child behaves worst in particular situations or places, or with particular other children or staff members. Perhaps the child becomes disruptive during story time or very silly in front of certain helpers. You can 'break the cycle' of the difficult behaviour by avoiding the situation altogether for a while. A difficult behaviour can soon become a habit, and it is helpful to set up the situation differently so that the habit is broken for a while. It also helps everyone, child and staff alike, feel more relaxed and confident about things. You are not being defeated in this; it is clever management because you should then have a plan to move the child towards the stage when he or she *can* cope without misbehaving. For example, if a child cannot tolerate close proximity from certain other children without fighting them, you can distract the child away from those children for a while but later set up structured and supported play activities where you are helping the child learn other ways of playing together.

Distract rather than confront

Distraction is one of the most powerful tools we have for managing young children's behaviour. Just at the moment when a squabble is brewing, we direct their attention to a new exciting event or opportunity, defusing the situation altogether. Again, do not feel you are sidestepping the issue; it is clever management to use distraction in early years settings. Again, note 'problem times' and plan other opportunities for helping the children learn more appropriate ways of behaving.

Make sure the activity suits the child's developmental level

So often, children who are referred to support services with behaviour difficulties turn out to be experiencing difficulties in learning as well. It is also true that many children are seen to have behaviour problems simply because the expectations on them were too high. A classic example is the tall, rather active and boisterous two-year-old who is perceived by adults to be older than he is. If you respond to his behaviour as you would a four-year-old, that child is going to find it hard to get things right. Another example would be a child who has not yet learned how to concentrate for longer than a minute or two, but who is expected to sit at a table and complete a worksheet.

Get full attention before giving directions

If necessary, bend down to the child's level, say the child's name, or gently touch his or her chin to ensure eye contact before giving instructions. Young children find it hard to realise that instructions given to a whole group also mean *them*, so you need to cue individual children in first to what you are about to say. Very active children tend to act without thinking, and you will need to teach looking skills and listening skills before you can expect the children to pay attention to what you are saying.

Give more positive attention before the trouble happens

Many children who appear to *seek* a lot of attention genuinely *need* a great deal of positive attention. Look for ways of providing that attention when these children are behaving appropriately (they do not have to be *especially* good) and target their praise specifically – 'Thank you for sharing the dough, Sam!' You may find that certain children behave more appropriately for some staff than others, and this might be because other staff members give more attention to misdemeanours than to appropriate behaviour.

Give a warning of changes of activity

Young children get so engrossed in what they are doing and have not learned to attend to more than one thing at a time. It can be very helpful if you give regular warnings about what is about to happen, so that the children have a chance to prepare themselves for a change of activity – 'Nearly time to tidy up now – then you can play outside'. Some settings put on particular pieces of music to signal impending transition times.

Anticipate problem times and be a step ahead

Difficult behaviours often occur when children are in a 'vacuum' between activities or waiting for something to happen, such as at 'going home time'. Make sure the children know not only what they can be doing now, but what they can do next. Helping children to plan and review their activities is a useful strategy here. You can also use visual timetables (a sequence of photographs illustrating the key activities and routines of the session) as a way of focussing certain children on what comes next. If a child with poor listening skills finds group story time difficult, then plan ahead by asking a helper to take her into the book corner for an individual story time. Gradually increase the number of children there until that child can listen within a larger group.

Give clear directions

Children need full reasons and explanations if they are to learn about their worlds, yet there may be times when that is not appropriate. Choose what you want to say, for example, *'No kicking'* and repeat that over, making the rule simple and clear. This is sometimes known as the broken record approach! Sometimes, the more that you elaborate, the more attention you are giving the child for behaving inappropriately. Instead, look for other times of day when you can talk together about reasons for behaving in a certain way and learn about behaving kindly.

Show the child what to do as well as saying it

Young children are usually too absorbed in what they are doing to respond to adult directions from across the room. If you are working with young children whose attention is short, approach these children and *model* to them what to do. These children might also find adult language difficult to understand, so add meaning to your words by showing children what to do as well. For example, if a child throws the toys into the box at tidy-up time, show that child how to make a game of 'parking' the cars gently, or putting the musical instruments back so that not a sound is made.

Choose a few simple rules and stick to them

These are especially useful when the children have contributed to them too, perhaps as a circle time activity. Stick to three to four rules at the most, perhaps relating to not hurting others, to being kind and to listening. Spend time with the children talking together about what it means to be kind and to help.

Changing the action

You can also plan interventions that directly affect the child's behaviour, as the following sections describe.

Stop it if you can

Some behaviours can be anticipated ahead and stopped from happening. If you know ahead that a lively child is going to join your setting who tends to behave impulsively and has little sense of danger, then you would make sure that your boundaries, doors and gates were totally secure. You might need to fit safety locks to certain cupboards and you would carry out a risk assessment of how safe your setting was, making sure that safety features such as electric plug covers were all in place. You can also take a look at the way your spaces are organised. Wide open spaces with wheeled toys call out to lively children to move at great speed. Consider how you can draw their attention towards the near distance rather than the far distance by dividing up the space, adding 'road' lines, making suggestions to channel their play.

Teach the child a new behaviour opposite to the first

When a child is playing constructively with another child on the car mat, he cannot at the same time be fighting. In other words, some behaviours are incompatible with others. You can use this fact to great advantage. Decide ahead what behaviours you wish to see in place of the problem behaviour, and then set this as a target for teaching. Suddenly you have a positive plan of action and are not focusing entirely on the negative behaviour. For example, you might decide to work hard to build up a child's level of concentration, to help him or her play in a supervised group or alongside another child. In other words, you are managing the difficult behaviour by delivering social skills training.

Praise another behaviour incompatible with the first

Sometimes, a child is already demonstrating appropriate and friendly behaviour as well as the difficult behaviour. This gives you a clear starting point for the child's behaviour management. Use all the approaches already discussed to plan situations which make the problem behaviour less likely to happen, and then selectively praise and give attention at times when the child is behaving appropriately. There will still be good times and bad times, but usually the proportion of good times steadily increases.

Changing the responses

The third option is to plan interventions which change the consequences of a child's behaviour, making it less likely to occur in the future.

Be absolutely consistent

This is the most difficult part of behaviour management. If they are to work effectively, you need to be consistent in your approaches. You can feel confused by a child's difficult behaviour and it is tempting to try one approach and then switch to another when it does not work immediately. You need to draw up a plan and to stick to it for at least three weeks. If a child hits, kicks or bites, then the same response must happen every single time, whoever the person supervising and whatever the situation. Otherwise, the children will learn that they can behave in a certain way if they make enough fuss or if they choose their audience or their timing.

Reward when the child is not doing the inappropriate behaviour

As well as focusing on the behaviour to be changed, you will need to think of a list of behaviours which the child would be showing when behaving appropriately instead. These behaviours should be both noticed and rewarded by you. For example, if you are planning an approach to stop Jed from biting, then you might note that whenever Jed was sitting at a table activity, or whenever he was sharing the water play, he did not bite. You should then give attention and praise Jed for playing well at these times. When praising appropriate behaviour, you should focus on the positive behaviour – 'Well done for sharing!' – and not on the negative; 'Well done for not biting'!

Biting

Pen picture

Jed is two. He is settled happily into his day nursery which he joined two months ago. Recently, Jed has started to bite other children. At first, staff thought this would be a passing phase but the behaviour is becoming worse. He seems to make a bee-line for certain other children and, unless he is caught in time, will bite so hard that it draws blood. Other children are becoming frightened of Jed and do not want to play near him. Other parents are beginning to complain.

How staff worked out what to do

Staff decided to start with an observation of when the attempts to bite were at their worst. An extra pair of hands was arranged so that one of them could become an observer for an hour. Jed's regular helpers were asked to watch out for him and step in using their usual approaches if he attempted to bite. They noticed that Jed was happy to play alone but was not happy when other children approached or tried to share his toys. This is when he would attempt to bite. He would also bite if he wanted a toy that another child was already holding – especially if he knew that they would not resist. Staff used their general observations and records to decide that there were no other concerns about his development, which appeared to be ahead of his age in everything expect social skills and social interaction. His language was coming

(*Continued*)

When behaviour needs to change

(Continued)

on well, though he sometimes became impatient with himself. After sharing their concerns with Jed's parents, staff realized that Jed had not had many experiences of playing socially with other children in the past. Jed is the only child in his family and was described by his parents as 'a determined character'.

What they did

Staff members decided to do two things. They decided to plan activities that would be enjoyable to Jed in which they played alongside him with one other child. They chose activities that were more fun when played with more than one child and taught Jed how to share, take turns and ask for things. Staff did this by giving clear instructions, showing him what to do as well as telling him and using strong praise and enthusiasm when he followed the rules. At other times of day, they decided to watch him carefully and step in to reiterate the simple rules if another child approached his play. If he attempted to bite, they gave a clear 'no biting', spoken with firmness and confidence but no anger. He was then removed apart from the other child, who was comforted. Jed would then be helped to say, 'Sorry' (his helper would say it for him at first) and redirected on to another activity.

Why it worked

Children bite for many reasons – anger, frustration (especially if they cannot yet talk), because it works, because it gets them attention, because they enjoy it, because they are teething or hungry and even out of passion. The observation helped staff work out that Jed was biting because he didn't know how to share or ask for things nicely, and that he hadn't yet learned the benefits of playing socially. Rather than give him plenty of attention for the biting, they set up activities that would be even more interesting and used these to actually teach Jed how to play socially. Had they tried to manage the behaviour using negative means – nagging him or being cross – Jed, being a determined child, might have continued with the behaviour just to keep life interesting. When he did try to bite, he discovered that more attention went to the other child and that saying sorry meant that everyone could move on.

Ignore attention-seeking behaviour where safe to do so

If a child is constantly swearing as a means of gaining a reaction from you all, this can be embarrassing and difficult to manage. Experience tells us that swearing responds best to an ignoring approach, yet you might feel you must be seen to respond and correct it. Instead, try to make it fun to behave appropriately and encourage other children to ignore silliness. So often, children who show difficult behaviour have become used to gaining attention and reaction for behaving inappropriately rather than appropriately. Try to understand that you are in the business of changing the *balance* of attention so that it becomes more attention-getting and fun for the child to behave appropriately than to misbehave.

Star charts and stickers can also work well

These are usually most effective when a child is about four, but they can also be used with younger children if they help. They serve the purpose of letting children know that they are behaving appropriately at this moment in time and serve as a concrete recognition of their efforts. Therefore they should never be removed because in the next moment in time the child was behaving differently. Stickers should not be overused and can be faded out gradually as new patterns of behaviour become established.

A consultative approach

One way to support each other within your professional or support network is to use a consultative approach. Nowadays, this approach is often used by outside professionals working with the setting, or indeed a family. However, you can also adapt it as a way of helping you all develop clear language and thinking about a child's behaviour and explore ways forward that are going to help. You might decide to set aside a slot each week with your SENCO or manager to explore any concerns or difficulties with the child's behaviour. The aim is for you to explore a concern and reach a better understanding of what is going on by using joint problem-solving. This should help you work out more effective approaches and strategies, based on the child's individual strengths.

Planning a behaviour consultation

Take the following steps when planning a behaviour consultation about a child:

- Find a quiet area where you will not be disturbed at a time when you can switch off your mobile phones.
- Agree on a time limit to discuss each child – perhaps 15 or 20 minutes.
- Make sure that those who know the child best will be present.
- Adapt the 'Behaviour consultation' box below to direct the discussion, and record your discussion.

Behaviour consultation

Name of child:
Date of consultation:
Who was present?

(*Continued*)

(*Continued*)

> What is the behaviour you are worried about?
> What concerns you about this child's behaviour?
> What approaches have you tried so far?
> What effects have you noticed?
> How would you like things to change?
> Are there other factors you think might be important?
> How are parents and carers involved?
> How can we work with them to support this child's behaviour?
> Is there any other agency involved?
> What will we do about the problem?
> When will we meet to talk about this again?

The first behaviour consultation

- Help each other put into words what it is you are concerned about and why. It helps if you can use clear unambiguous words to do this. Find phrases which are not judgemental in any way (this takes skill and practice).
- Talk about what approaches have been tried so far. The very fact that you are meeting regularly in this way encourages you all to see behaviour not simply as a problem to be spotted and identified, but as a challenge to be worked on.
- Ask yourselves what you have noticed following these interventions. Listen to one another, as you might all have noticed different things. You might pick up some clues as to why some staff might have less success than others without feeling threatened about this.
- Ask yourselves how you would like things to change, and begin to talk about how this might be done, building on your knowledge and experience of the child and what you know to be good practice.
- Explore whether there might be other factors you think might be important, such as home factors or medical issues.
- Talk about how parents and carers are involved and how they might be feeling about it all. Decide how you will work together with them to effect the change.
- Make a note of any other agency involved and what their input has been or might be in the future.
- Make sure you end up with clear conclusions, strategies and actions and that everyone understands what these are.

- Keep a record of your discussion – even if your interventions do not work out, this will form part of your 'evidence' of how you have planned to meet the child's needs in the past, in case you come to need more outside professional support in the future.
- Allow three weeks for the interventions to be effective (behaviours often appear to get worse before they improve) and discuss again then.

Children with additional support needs

Sometimes a child's behaviour strikes you as very different to usual, or it becomes so difficult to manage that you run out of your usual approaches and interventions. You might need to plan more specialist approaches with the involvement of an outside agency such as an educational or child psychologist, social worker or member of the CAMHS team (Child and Adolescent Mental Health Service). Hopefully, your SENCO can advise you or will know of local support systems for outside advice. There are also some children whose SEN have already been identified who have certain recognized conditions such, as ASD or AD/HD, that affect their behaviour long-term. It helps if you can have a general understanding of how these particular conditions might lead to children behaving differently, and this is covered in the next chapter.

Reference

Mortimer, H. (2006) *Behaviour Management in the Early Years*. Stafford: QEd Publications.

7 | Children who behave 'differently': Special educational needs and disability

Not all children follow the usual pathway in developing their social skills and behaviour, and this is explored in Chapter 7. We consider children who behave 'differently' and who may therefore need approaches to support their special educational needs and disabilities (SEND).

Do we need to label?

This has been a knotty area for us all, and it is easy to feel muddled about it. Is it essential to spot these children and to diagnose them early so that we can give them the right label? The answer is that early identification of conditions such as autism is indeed essential – but it is a *medical* diagnosis and made by others. If we see our role in the early years foundation stage as one of spotting what is wrong with a child, then there is a danger that we put our interventions on hold whilst we await a diagnosis, and not get on with the job that we as early years practitioners have to do – that of focusing on what the child's special educational needs (SEN) are and how to support them. Time is precious. In the ideal world, all the professionals should be joining up their work as a team around the child, and practitioners should be working alongside others to identify the child's needs (which might or might not lead to a medical diagnosis) and plan how best to support the child in the setting. So labelling might be important in certain conditions – but we as practitioners do not require this in order to get on with what we need to do.

From a medical point of view, labelling becomes part of defining a *disability*. A disability, under the Equality Act 2010, means that there is a physical or mental impairment which has a long-term (likely to be a year or more) and substantial (more than minor or trivial) adverse effect on the ability to carry out normal day-to-day activities. If a child is disabled, we must not discriminate against him or her in any way, and we must make reasonable adjustments to ensure the child is not put at a disadvantage.

Now let us think about parents and carers and the question of labelling. Some parents and carers find it so much easier to cope with the fact that their child is different in some way if they have a diagnosis or label. Having a label allows them to move on and gives them a definite job to do in order to understand and support their child. Other parents shy away from the labelling process, and, if they feel under pressure about it, they can lose trust with professionals. Each family is unique.

As one of the professionals who knows a child best, you are well placed to support families through any process of diagnosis. You will read more about the stages that parents and carers often describe in coming to terms with the labelling process in Chapter 8. When parents are anxious or ambiguous about going for a specialist referral, I often use this kind of approach. I might say, 'As you know, we have found out that Jessie might be learning and behaving in a way that might be right on the edge of the autistic spectrum. We know that children on the autistic spectrum find it easiest when ... and so let's plan our support in this way . ... We can see if this approach seems to make sense for Jessie. We will meet again to see how effective our approaches have been and talk again about whether it would be helpful to ask for further assessment'.

Special educational needs

Some children with disabilities will not have special educational needs. Jacob was born with one of his arms significantly shortened – this will mean special adaptations and adjustments throughout his life – yet he manages beautifully at nursery and there is very little that he cannot do compared to his peers. Other children may have special educational needs but not be disabled. Bertie has a difficulty in forming verbal concepts and a speech and language therapist is working with practitioners to help his language development; in the long term, he is expected to manage well. However, many children with disabilities will also have special educational needs and, with respect to behaviour, the most common disabilities or medical conditions in this category are autistic spectrum disorder (ASD) and attention deficit with or without hyperactivity (AD/HD) conditions.

Children are described as having special educational needs if they have a learning difficulty or disability which calls for special educational provision to be made for them. For these children, we must plan approaches which are substantially 'additional or different' to the usual ones. Note that children do not have SEN simply because they have been diagnosed with a condition. They are described as having SEN only if they do not respond to your usual levels of support and therefore require approaches which are additional or different to usual; it is a pragmatic definition.

You can see that some children's behaviour might be related to a long-term disability (such as those who have been diagnosed with ASD or AD/HD) and others might require additional or different approaches because their behaviour gets in the way of their learning appropriately at this stage of their development (such as those who have a severe attachment disorder). Under SEN guidance, children might be described as presenting with 'social, emotional and mental health difficulties', and our additional and different approaches can be planned because they are needed, rather than as a result of a label.

Children who behave 'differently'

The rest of this chapter will explore what it means to be learning and behaving in a way that is autistic or suggests a significant attention difficulty. Suddenly, we are back on familiar territory, because we are talking about needs and are not waiting for whether or not a child will be given 'the' diagnosis.

Working with children who have autistic spectrum difficulties

The first thing to say is that each child is unique, and you are well placed to get to know each child as an individual with their own particular profile of strengths and weaknesses. For some children, early language and communication skills do not develop spontaneously. Perhaps the child appears to be developing normally for the first year or so, and then communication and language skills seem to come to a halt. These children tend to become absorbed into their own worlds and agendas. They may use little eye contact or even struggle to avoid it. They may join in an activity only if an adult insists and helps them. They tend not to play interactively and cooperatively with other children. They may seem aloof and indifferent to other people, preferring certain favourite objects, toys or videos. If they need something, then they tend to lead an adult's hand towards it rather than to make requests.

Children with autism sometimes develop speech very slowly. Others may talk incessantly and be adept at remembering whole passages or rhymes or at 'collecting' facts or labels for things. Their conversations, when they develop, can be one-sided and the children find it hard to take on board the listener's point of view, talking about what is on their mind when the listener has no idea what it is. They may not wait for gaps in conversations before butting in, position themselves unusually when conversing, find it hard to regulate the volume and tone of their voices and talk 'at' you rather than 'to' you. They may carry out little routines and rituals of behaviours in order to 'keep the world the same', and they find changes to routines difficult to cope with. Their play tends to be repetitive and stereotyped, with little creativity or imagination.

To draw this together, children with ASD have challenges in the following:

- Understanding social and emotional information relating to others
- Understanding and using all aspects of communication, regardless of speech development
- Monitoring, controlling and being flexible in both thinking and behaving (Jordan, 2002).

This is known as the *triad of impairments*, and children need to have significant and long-term difficulties in all three areas if they are going to receive a diagnosis. Thus you may have many children with rather 'quirky' behaviour in your setting who may respond well to the approaches we are going to think about, but they will not necessarily require specialist assessment and further diagnosis. Autism is called a spectrum because there are a wide range of difficulties which affect different children in different ways. They may have problems with social relationships, with communication, with developing imagination and play, and be resistant to changes in routine. It is usually seen as a lifelong disability and early diagnosis and help is known to be vital. There can be quite a gap between the adults in a child's life starting to feel concerned and an actual diagnosis (usually by a specialist multidisciplinary team) and so it helps for early years educators to have these general approaches in their toolbox of support.

Supporting young children with ASD

What can early practitioners do to support children whose behaviour appears to lie somewhere on the autistic spectrum? Dip into these approaches to see which are effective for the children you support. We will divide our approaches four ways – how to work with the children's particular strengths, how to support their weaknesses, how to look for promising opportunities to promote their development and how to meet the challenges when their behaviour becomes tricky to manage. You will meet this format again when we look at children who might have AD/HD later in the chapter.

Working with strengths

Children who have ASD are often very visual learners who respond well to visual and pictorial information. They also feel secure when there are clear routines and procedures and this is something that you can build on. Indeed, they tend to be very literal and 'black and white' in their understanding, and so, with the right rules, they will usually try to be compliant (if they understand what the rule is). Many also have particular areas of special interest and fascination and it helps to tap into these when planning activities and play opportunities.

Clear expectations

As with all children, those with ASD can behave totally different in different settings because the expectations on them are different. If you expect a child not to communicate, then that is what you are likely to experience. If you know that a child can communicate given time and opportunity, then use pause, prompts and slow the exchange down so that an answer is clearly expected.

Encourage communication

At first, encourage and reinforce all attempts by the child with ASD to communicate, even if the timing and content are not entirely appropriate. For most children, communication opens the door to exciting social interchange – for the child with ASD this is not necessarily so. You would not wish to put them off just at the point that they are trying it out. If language skills have already developed, give the child a stock phrase to use if he or she does not understand something (for example, 'Say it again') – this can reduce everyone's frustration.

Familiar routine

If the child understands language, use familiar, everyday situations to talk about sharing, taking turns and understanding what other children might be thinking. Try to keep to a familiar and structured routine. Children with ASD find it hard to understand time sequences and they sometimes become anxious about what will happen next. For some children, this makes it hard for them to finish one activity since they are not sure how to start the next. They might become locked in to very repetitive play in a bid to keep their world safe and predictable; show them how to move on.

Giving feedback

Children with ASD need regular feedback on how they are behaving. Target your feedback directly to the child and make it specific: for example, 'Patrick is *helping* Mrs Willis, thank you' or 'Rosie is *sitting down*. Good.'

Good role models

Once a pupil with ASD has learned to imitate, you can use this to advantage when teaching social skills. However, imitating good role models will not be effective on its own unless the pupil with ASD is also talked through what is happening: for example, 'Look, Amber, Laura is *asking* for the pencil and *smiling* when Rea gives it to her. You try – *ask* … now *smile* … well done, Amber!' Often this will mean putting children in different groups for different types of activity in order to get the best out of everyone.

Musical interactions

Many children with ASD love music and movement. You can use music time to encourage them to look, listen and join in. You might find that a 'music makers' approach (Chapter 2; Mortimer, 2008) is a useful way of planning activities which are precisely targeted for the child who has ASD, but are also appropriate for all the children in the early years foundation stage; that is the joy of using creative activities such as music.

Special responsibilities

Even though children with ASD tend to lack self-consciousness, you can still make good use of giving them special responsibilities in the setting. These give the child with ASD

Meet Richie

This is my first music makers session at a large 100-place town nursery, with children in two large prefabricated huts according to their age. I am given the three- to four-year-olds: about thirty of them with four adults who do not look at all confident with the proceedings.

Richie is running around, shouting and jumping off the tables. He has recently been diagnosed as having autism. His parents are understandably upset and extremely tense. Perhaps partly for this reason, Richie's behaviour has almost been beyond control during the last few days. It is his father who has brought him today.

I start with a warm-up song. Most of the children look happy and watch carefully. The adults still look unsure and do not sing. Richie is held on his dad's knee and immediately goes into full struggle and scream, beating his father and shouting silly music. We battle on. He escapes. I explain to his father that I would like to see him go his own way to see if I can attract him with the music. Dad tells me, 'You'll be lucky'. We try again. The children are joining in with a clapping song, and the adults 'unfreezing'.

We sing the greeting song. Richie stops at his name and looks at me, smiling. He runs off again. We sing a wobbly jelly song. The children are now attending beautifully, with the exception of Richie. Merle has severe speech and language delay and is watching attentively, joining in the actions. Ben 'never sits still' and has attention difficulties; he is watching me closely and following the clues.

I lay the percussion instruments out on the floor, asking the children to wait until I have finished before choosing, and (just as I am about to invite him to choose first) Richie darts in and grabs the largest drum and a stick. He takes it to underneath a side table away from the group and is absorbed in beating it. We all play; I tell the children to play when I play and stop when I stop. We have a few goes. They all look and listen for my piano accordion attentively, even those with listening difficulties.

I then explain we will start when Richie starts and stop when Richie stops. After two goes of this, Richie looks up at me with a full and almost startling eye contact. He drums furiously and stops. We all join in loudly. He smiles. He gives one soft tap. We copy. He plays a long string. We copy. By this time, he is grinning and I feel in full reciprocal communication with him. He looks playful for a moment as he sees just how quiet he can be, and we still hear him and copy. This carries on for a full five minutes. Richie is leading the band. Dad is smiling for the first time.

We start to march around Richie and his drum. When I halt, everyone stops, and we do not start until Richie beats his drum again. This takes us to the end of the twenty minutes. Richie occasionally runs off some steam but then returns to his drum.

(*Continued*)

(Continued)

> **Thinking point**
>
> - Was this one of those 'ta-da!' moments (Chapter 2)?
> - What exactly was Richie doing for the very first time ever that made everyone so proud?

very appropriate prestige in front of the other children, can assist inclusion if managed carefully and allow you all to benefit from any exceptional skills and interests that the child with ASD might have.

Useful requests

In the early stages of development, in order to help children with ASD communicate with you, you need to encourage them to *show* you what they want. You need to make it a little bit difficult for them to get what they want so that they learn to communicate at whatever level they are capable of. If a child can simply get a drink by wandering off and helping him- or herself, what need has that child to communicate? But if you anticipate what the children want and offer a simple choice, then you are expecting them to point or reach for their choice. This is a very early stage of communicating and can be built on for children who have very little language. Later, you can expect an approximation of the word 'drink', such as 'di'. You can use this approach before rough-and-tumble play too. Many children with ASD love physical play and repetitive games. If you wait until you have the briefest of eye contact before repeating them, you have again taught them to begin to communicate what they want.

Visual timetables

You can help by showing the child pictures or symbols about what is happening next. Make a series of cards with Velcro backs which can be arranged in line on a felt board. Or use a white board or interactive screen to talk about and draw the session's timetable at its beginning. You can also help by providing the words for what the child is doing. Do this by providing a simple commentary about what is happening: for example, 'Joseph is writing', or 'Zoe is putting away'.

Widening their interests

Sometimes children with ASD have intense interests in certain items or topics. For example, they might be fascinated by trains and tracks. They might be intensely interested in switches and all things electrical. They might cling onto two oblong bricks and stare at these intently as they arrange them meticulously in line. They might insist on carrying a certain blue beaker everywhere. Try to be interested in *their* interests but introduce new things too. Provide a special place to put the beaker when the child is using hands for something else. Introduce cars to the train mat. Help the child extend the fascination in bricks to building and simple construction play. Try to support the child's activities, though to distract the child if he or she becomes too absorbed or obsessed with them.

Working with weaknesses

We looked earlier in the chapter at areas of particular difficulty that children with ASD often show. If you are already familiar with the times when the child is likely to feel more stressed, you can plan ahead to make the session easier for them.

Avoid ambiguity

Children with ASD find it hard to understand double meaning, sarcasm or irony and may interpret it too literally and become confused. Avoid requests such as, 'Would you like to do your painting now?' (The honest answer might be 'No!', and, for a child with ASD, this would not be cheekiness!) Replace this with '*Rowan* – time to wash hands *now*'. If children with ASD begin to echo what you have said or resort to repetitive behaviour, this could be a sign that they have not understood you and are beginning to feel stressed. Make sure that your instructions are concrete, direct and explicit, and support these with picture prompts or actions if you need to.

Being patient

You may need to wait longer than usual before a child responds to what you have asked for. Give a child with ASD time to respond or to imitate before you come in with a repetition or the answer. Sometimes these children need longer than usual to process what you have just said or shown them before they can then put together their response. Sometimes signing is used in order to make instructions and requests clearer.

Careful questioning

Questions often confuse children with ASD. They may not understand the question word itself (what/why/where/when) and they find it hard to handle open-ended questions. Where possible, turn questions into statements with a pause at the appropriate moment – 'The colour of the leaves is …' rather than 'What colour are the leaves?' You might also find the child echoing back a questions such as, 'Do you want the scissors?' when they really mean, 'I want the scissors'. You need to recognise the intent in the words and be ready to oblige with your own restatement: 'Oh – you want the scissors. Here you are'.

Developing scripts

Children with ASD are often at a loss as to what to say in certain social situations and may end up disrupting them instead. Use your observations to identify these situations and help the child rehearse what to say (for example, how to ask another child to lend something, how to ask someone to play with them, what to say on arrival and departure). In a similar way, you can make up stories to illustrate a social point and use them to demonstrate to the child with ASD how to behave in that situation. Remember to support generalisation of the behaviour to new situations, since this may not happen naturally.

Distraction

When it comes to obsessive behaviour, you will already know when the child with ASD is most likely to need the security of their repetitive behaviour. You soon begin to see a pattern of stress or lack of structure leading to an increase in repetitive mannerisms. Plan ahead for difficult times by distracting the child with ASD with something different, and making it clear to the child what is going to happen next in the session.

Engaging attention

Children with autistic difficulties are often felt to be deaf, because they pay little attention to spoken instructions. Use their name clearly, get down to their level, try to encourage eye contact albeit briefly (to signal your intent to communicate) and then speak. Encourage but do not actually insist upon eye contact (since for some children it makes them too anxious and prevents them from thinking clearly). When you are issuing instructions to the whole group, address the child with ASD by name first to engage attention. Give very clear and simple messages, showing the child as well as telling him or her what to do.

Keep it concrete

Children with ASD often have problems in understanding personal pronouns such as 'me' and 'you'. It is often helpful to use real names at first, such as 'Give it to Molly' rather than 'Give it to me'. They also have difficulties in understanding abstract language and will need concrete and visual props when learning new concepts.

Picture exchange

Sometimes children are taught to exchange pictures or symbols in order to make their needs known more clearly (such as using PECS – the Picture Exchange Communication System).

Social skills training

Just as children with ASD can learn rules for general behaviour, they will need you to help them learn the rules of social interaction. Children with ASD may need to be taught social skills directly, because they cannot pick up incidentally all the subtle clues needed to manage a social exchange. The focus of your approach should be on telling the child what to do rather than what not to do. You can actually practise where to stand when holding a conversation, and what tone and volume of voice to use for different situations.

Teach turn-taking

It is well worthwhile to spend time teaching turn-taking in small groups or with partners. Even if a child with ASD mastered this at home, the skill can change as soon as there is a new situation or new people involved. Start with simple reciprocal play involving 'my turn – your turn' (such as pouring sand over each other's hands, rolling a ball between you or blowing and bursting bubbles).

Transition objects

Children with ASD sometimes have a genuine difficulty in moving from one area to another – for example, coming from home into the setting. By giving them a transition object (such as something to give to the key person, or a cushion to sit on at group time) you can calm these moments down for them. Giving children a definite job to do in a new situation helps in a similar way (such as hanging your jacket on the caterpillar sign).

Making use of the key person

Start by helping the child feel settled when learning one-to-one with a key person. Children with ASD tend to find adults more predictable and therefore secure than other children at first. For younger children, that worker can begin by simply working or playing in parallel to the child, observing how they are behaving, placing objects of interest nearby and gently leading the child when new instructions are needed (such as for outdoor playtime). As the adult becomes familiar with the child's routines and behaviours, it becomes possible for that person to predict what the child will do next. You begin to see the world through the child's eyes. Gradually involve one or more other children in the work or play, staying close to support and assist. Because you now have a feel of what the child will do, it will be possible for you to interpret the child's play to other children and thus include them in the play. You are acting as a bridge for the child and helping the child become more sociable.

Working with opportunities

You met Richie earlier in the chapter and saw how we were able to make the most of his response to music by creating a golden opportunity for him to interact reciprocally with the other children. Here are some ways of spotting moments when you can step in to make the most of a child's learning, despite the child's ASD.

Catch the moment

You need to spend time teaching a child with ASD how to recognise feelings and emotions in themselves and others. The most effective way to do this is to catch the moment when the child is clearly emotional and then interpret this for them, linking cause and effect: for example, 'Jordan was working. Ross took her pens. Jordan is unhappy'. Later, you can use this kind of approach to talk about how a child *would* feel if such-and-such happened.

Game plan

For children at an early stage of social communication, try this approach. Spend ten minutes a session playing alongside them with an identical toy or piece of equipment to the one they are currently absorbed in. Copy what they are doing. When they begin to notice what you are doing, move in to work or play with them, sharing the same object. Again, copy their actions. The idea is to encourage them to see that *their* behaviour is resulting in *your* behaviour. You can then begin to play turn-taking games such as setting up and knocking down skittles.

Interpretation

Sometimes children with ASD give out negative social signals to other children without meaning to and this can add to their isolation. Use your knowledge of the child and how he or she behaves to interpret their behaviour to other children when necessary: for example, 'George didn't mean to push you – that's his way of telling you that he would love to play tag with you' or 'Sara didn't mean to scream at you – she hasn't learned yet how to tell you that she is very busy and can't be disturbed at the moment'.

Social stories

If a child with ASD is finding a particular social situation tricky, try writing a social story. Social stories were developed by Carol Gray (2000) to help teach social skills to children and others with autism. They are short descriptions of a particular situation, event or activity, which includes specific information about what to expect and why. The goal is to teach social understanding over rote compliance, and to describe rather than to direct. There is a clear format to follow, and they are tailor-made for each child and each situation.

Use structure

Children with ASD can find it hard to cope with free play or open learning situations. When there is no clear structure, they might begin to behave inappropriately or retreat into repetitive or rigid behaviours. If you can be aware of this, it is helpful if you can introduce some structure even to free times. Offer clear choices of what to do next.

Working with challenges

You work in a social setting and there are bound to be challenges for children who find social interaction and social understanding somewhat of a mystery. Many of the techniques you considered in Chapter 6 will also be helpful when supporting a young child with ASD.

Broken record

Try not to elaborate and explain more and more each time a child with ASD does not comply with a direct request. This is likely to overload them with language. Instead, simply repeat the same instruction over and over, if necessary showing the child what to do as well as telling them – this is known as the *broken record* technique. Keep language short and simple, emphasising key words.

Avoiding situations

Carry out a STAR observation (Chapter 6) and it may become obvious to you that you could alleviate a particular problem significantly by avoiding certain situations. For example, you could arrange for the child to miss plenary times for a while and work in a smaller group situation instead.

Motivators

One of the challenges in teaching young children with ASD is that they may not be motivated by social rewards alone. Praise might be meaningless, your gaze might be unsettling to them and the chance to play with other children might be something definitely to be avoided. Therefore we sometimes use more concrete motivators for children with ASD, such as a favourite item to collect or a 'Well done!' picture card. Always pair these with social praise so that, in time, the child comes to see the praise as rewarding as well. Make sure the play activity itself is intrinsically motivating for a child with ASD by appealing to any appropriate areas of interests (such as dinosaurs or trains) when selecting topics, themes and tasks. Usually, these children need individually designed play opportunities at first in order to play within their areas of interest and get them going. You can add extra motivators that can be used as tokens for good behaviour – stickers, a favourite activity or time with a favourite plaything.

Removing distractions

You may find it easiest to play with just one toy or activity at a time, putting all other materials well out of sight. Try to reduce the number of options available, such as starting to complete a number puzzle with just the last three pieces of information missing.

In order to give the child the idea that they can have *choice*, show two activities or toys and ask the child to reach for or touch the one to be played with next.

Safe base

Provide a quiet 'safe base' where the child can go if they are feeling overloaded or stressed. Children with autistic difficulties quickly feel stressed and anxious if there are many people about or if the demands on them are too great. If there is too much stimulation of any kind, they might revert to repetitive behaviours just to make the world predictable again. Once you have got to know the child, you will be able to see when the child is feeling stressed and move to your quiet area to wind down. It is also important at some stage of the child's day for him or her to have time to be alone and to engage in a preferred activity of the child's own choosing.

Warnings

Children with ASD find it hard to switch quickly into someone else's agenda. Give a warning before a change in activity (for example, 'It will be home time in five minutes so finish off now'), perhaps playing a particular piece of music to signal 'tidy up time'. If the child has little concept of the passage of time, use an egg timer to signal the remaining time. Egg timers can also be used to encourage fair turn-taking at the computer.

Children with attention deficit disorders

ADD (attention deficit disorder) and ADHD (the same, but with hyperactivity) are medical terms, and specialists have clear guidelines for diagnosing them. Although all young children have short attention spans and are often very active, there are some children who have significant difficulties when compared with their peers the same age which affect

- sustaining their attentions,
- controlling impulsive behaviour, and
- controlling their motor activity.

These difficulties can affect their learning, their behaviour and their developmental progress. We will use the general term 'AD/HD' when talking about children with these diagnoses. The conditions are recognised more widely in the United States, and there is still controversy about using the label and around the whole issue of prescribing stimulant medication to children. Most NHS Trusts now have clearly defined protocols for diagnosing and treating AD/HD. The reason that medication is not generally available for younger children is that it has very different effects on different individuals. A child needs to have developed the introspection necessary for being able to report, 'This is how it makes me feel'. Otherwise, we might fail to observe what can be quite unpleasant side effects for the child. Many doctors would not consider prescribing medication until the child is at least six; we would normally use behavioural management approaches for these children.

What you might observe

Children with AD/HD or attention difficulties may have some or many of the following characteristics (adapted from Mortimer, 2002):

- They have attention difficulties which are *much greater than for other children their age* and which have persisted for more than six months in different situations.
- They find it hard to listen to stories or to concentrate for more than a minute or so on any one play activity.
- They find it hard to respond to spoken instructions, forgetting what you have said from one moment to the next.
- They may behave impulsively, rushing into something without any thought of the consequences.
- They might behave in an almost random manner until you step in to stop them, lacking any internal control.
- They might find it extremely difficult to sit still or to keep to their own spaces, especially when sitting on the floor or waiting in line.
- They may seem almost driven by high physical energy, always on the go, climbing, running, rushing, fiddling, touching, talking, shouting.
- They may fail to build on their learning and play, continuing in a rather random and aimless manner.
- They may have poor confidence and low self-esteem.

Useful strategies for children with attention difficulties

Working with strengths

Children with significant attention difficulties often have amazing levels of energy and enthusiasm and it helps to tap into this. Interestingly, some children focus best when they can run around and be active from time to time, and others find it easiest to settle if they stay calm. You will need to use your observations to experiment with what works best for the child you are working with.

Avoiding repetition

Try to avoid repetitive tasks which might become boring. Although it is helpful to have the general daily routine predictable and safe, look for new and interesting ways of playing and learning within that structure which are going to have an element of novelty and stimulation.

Introduce the words

Children with attention difficulties benefit greatly from the chance to talk with you ahead of any activity, to plan it together and then to review what they have done and how it worked afterwards. This use of 'plan–do–review' helps them to think about and engage with their learning, which, in turn, helps the child become less impulsive and more reflective. Use your own running commentary as the child plays to hold their attention on what they are doing and to show that you value and are interested in their actions. This is far more effective than constant questioning.

Working with weaknesses

Children with significant attention difficulties find it very hard to focus on one thing for long or to resist other distractions that come their way. If they also have hyperactivity, they may behave as if they had a coiled spring inside them or were driven by a motor – and this they cannot help. We support them best if we can plan the session and the environment in a way that makes it easier for them to focus and to learn, sandwiching active times with quieter times.

Avoid large group activities

Children with attention difficulties are likely to find it easiest to concentrate when playing in pairs rather than a large group. In this way, they do not become overstimulated and distracted. Often, their social skills are poor, and there can be too many demands placed on them when having to cope with a large group of others.

Breaking tasks down

Try to break tasks down into simpler steps so that the child with a short attention span can still play and learn from them. Keep your demands on the child short and simple to begin with; it might be a major step for the child to do *anything* which is not from their own agenda to begin with and this should be celebrated. Use your praise and your encouragement constantly to show the child that he or she is playing well.

Build up concentration

Look at how long the child can concentrate at present and aim to build this up, step by small step, until the child can concentrate for a short period of something of their choosing independently. Later, you can extend this to short tasks of your choosing. Make sure you have eye contact before you speak to the child and use the child's name to get attention. Give very clear, short and concrete directions, showing the child what to do as well as telling. Ask the child to repeat back what you have said and praise him or her for remembering.

Teach the concept of time

Sometimes, children with attention difficulties have great difficulties in understanding time sequences and also sequencing information. Talk about the time of day and introduce familiar times on the clock ('At 10 o'clock we have drinks ... at 12 o'clock we go home', etc.). Talk about what happened yesterday, today, tomorrow. Cut up story pictures and play at arranging these in sequence. Use a picture board to put up simple pictures representing what will happen during the session.

Working with opportunities

Outdoor play holds huge advantages for active learners. You can spot those 'ta-da!' moments by remaining one step ahead and providing plenty of attention when the child is managing to focus and comply. Your own attentions will inevitably be drawn to situations that have gone awry; instead you must tune yourselves to notice when a child with AD/HD is behaving on target.

Clear routines and boundaries

Children with short attention spans benefit from clear routines and structures so that they know what is going to happen and when. If attention is short, then these children sometimes find it helpful to 'sandwich' short periods of sustained concentration and effort with periods of time when they can be more active or have a free choice in their play. The best approach is therefore to start with very short periods of structured activity, moving step-by-small-step towards periods of longer concentration. Very strong encouragement and praise is needed to keep this fun, attention-getting and motivating for the child.

Quiet spaces

Children with attention difficulties or AD/HD may have a greater need than most children for a distraction-free space to work in for activities which require sustained concentration, looking or listening. Try to have a quiet area which you can withdraw to with a small group of children and use this *before* difficulties with behaviour arise rather than as a reaction to them. If a child needs time to cool off, find somewhere quiet to withdraw to and give minimal attention until the child is calm again and ready for you to talk together about what happened.

Staying positive

Do not be surprised if you have to give reminders constantly since the child might forget your instructions readily (or might not have paid attention to them in the first place). Try not to lose patience with the child; you might feel exasperated that you have to do so, but then you have already recognised that the child does have a genuine difficulty in attending so this should not be a surprise to you. Small and immediate rewards and praise are much more effective than larger rewards given at the end of a session. You can use favourite activities as effective rewards; 'When you have finished your painting, you can go on the computer ...' Always stay calm when you address any difficult behaviours, keeping your language simple and clear. If you become cross or upset, it will only stir the child up further and make it more difficult for the child to think logically and rationally about controlling his or her behaviour.

Working with challenges

All this means that you are likely to find yourself very busy! You have perhaps found yourself reacting more and more frequently to calamities, spills, tumbles, clashes of will, and are now finding that you need to make active plans for getting one step ahead. You might also have found yourself working hard to extend the child's play so that you can move on from the 'butterfly' stage of flitting from one activity to the next. You might have been tempted to see the child as misbehaving, though, on reflection, have realised that the child really cannot help it. Either way, you will probably be feeling that it is time to apply some structured interventions.

Managing challenging behaviour

Behaviour management (see Chapter 6) is a useful tool for using when planning changes in difficult behaviours. Because children with AD/HD find it hard to concentrate and attend, they often behave very impulsively and lack the social skills needed for social play and two-way give and take. Perhaps it is now time to make detailed observations, plan consistent interventions and evaluate your progress. Focus on the child's behaviour without making them believe they are the 'naughty' one.

Supporting parents and carers

AD/HD can be viewed as a 'hidden disability' since it is so often seen as wilful problem of self-control rather than as a disability. Parents who suspect difficulties are often told to wait and see, though without support, the child's difficulties can become worse. The likelihood is that, if you are seeing that the child has considerable difficulties in behaving in the setting, there are likely to be difficulties at home as well. Remind parents that they are not on their own. Simply showing the parents or carers that you understand that the child has genuine difficulties and that you do not see the child as being wilfully naughty can be a great support to them. Without making it seem as though you are the experts, share strategies that prove to be successful between home and setting so that you can actually help to improve everybody's life. In the next chapter, we explore ways in which you can support each other and support parents and carers through some of these potentially stressful times.

References

Gray, C. (2000) *The New Social Story Book: Illustrated Edition*. Arlington, TX: Future Horizons.
Jordan, R. (2002) *Autistic Spectrum Disorders in the Early Years*. Stafford: QEd.
Mortimer, H. (2002) *Supporting Children with AD/HD and Attention Difficulties in the Early Years*. Stafford: QEd Publications.
Mortimer, H. (2008) *Music makers: Music circle times to include everyone*. Revised Edition. Stafford: QEd Publications.
For information on PECS, visit www.pecs-unitedkingdom.com
For information on Social Stories and Carol Gray, visit www.autism.org.uk

8 Supporting parents, carers and each other

Managing challenging or 'different' behaviour can be a stressful time and Chapter 8 provides ideas for supporting parents, carers and each other. At the end of the day, all the ways that we have explored for understanding and reassuring young children also apply to those of us doing the caring, the teaching and the supporting.

When behaviour becomes stressful

Despite the pleasures and rewards of working with young children, it can be very stressful when you have to manage extremely challenging behaviour, day in and day out. All too easily, you can find yourself losing confidence, switching between approaches and putting off what you know to be the case: that sooner or later you are going to have to raise the matter with parents or carers. All sorts of emotions can be stirred up in us. Children's behaviour can make us feel angry, confused, distressed and, above all, guilty for the fact that we have not been able to manage it more effectively. All the principles relating to self-esteem and confidence covered earlier in this book apply equally well to us as adults, and it can be reassuring to understand that everybody will feel stressed at times.

It helps if we understand that stress is a normal part of working life and not a reflection of our particular ability to perform the job. Talk about stress openly and aim to be professionally supportive to each other. In this chapter, we introduce some of the strategies that can help and also look into how we can also support parents and carers better as they go through phases of their children's particularly difficult behaviour.

Seeing challenges differently

When a child's behaviour is particularly problematical, those of you who are trying to deal with it may already be feeling stressed, emotionally vulnerable and perhaps defensive. You may feel that you are being asked for 'the answer' and you may be left feeling frustrated and inadequate. All of these feelings can lead towards exclusion rather than inclusion of the child and the child's individual needs.

It can be helpful to bear these points in mind:

- There are no 'right answers' – only individual solutions.
- Therefore it helps to explore each situation and come up with the best ways forward.
- You will become a more effective manager of behaviour in the future if you reflect on the behaviour problem and work out tailor-made interventions yourself – so try not to rely exclusively on 'recipe book' approaches.

Throughout this book, you have met various individual solutions to real children and the real behaviours they were exhibiting in the boxed sections. By taking time to gain a pen picture of the child and his or her strengths and challenges first, and then reflecting on what might be done to support, you will have seen what the practitioners did, and why it probably worked well for everyone. You will never be sure; you can never state with confidence, 'I pressed this switch and that is what resulted – problem solved!' What you are actually doing is playing behaviour detective: you are working out why you think a particular behaviour is persisting and therefore what you might try in order to help. This is professional and insightful practice and is an example of *action research* in which you plan, do, evaluate and review. Also, if you can see challenging behaviour as a problem to be investigated rather than as a personal threat, it makes our role more intriguing and less stressful.

Stress management

Stress, anxiety and anger are closely linked because they share the same physiological reaction in our bodies. This reaction is sometimes called the *fight or flight* reaction and is chemically based and controlled by a complex and finely balanced system within the brain and the nervous system. As we evolved as hunters and gatherers, it was important for us to have a rapid mechanism that allowed us to see a beast and make a split-second decision as to whether to chase and attack it or whether to flee for our lives. It was no good pausing to think about it. This is why the emotional part of our brain is sometimes called the primitive area of the brain – it acts without logical thought and almost despite ourselves. We met the implications for brain development and babies' behaviour in Chapter 1.

Nowadays we may have evolved and developed much higher thinking skills, but our emotional brains continue to be vitally important for learning which things in life to avoid and which to approach and explore. Very young children are inevitably driven more by their emotional brains than their logical – they are all needs and reactions. However, in time, toddlers and young children develop the language and understanding to link their emotional feelings to their words and their experiences and thereby to develop *emotional literacy*.

The fact is that our emotional brains can switch in without us being fully aware of why or where the feelings are coming from. Some people talk about this phenomenon as forming part of our emotional intelligence – if we can understand where our feelings are coming from and what emotional experiences or 'luggage' have formed them, then we are emotionally intelligent individuals. We have explored in Chapters 1 and 3 how children's emotional needs are met and how the experiences they have gone through can affect how they handle emotional times and attachments later on in life. So, too, we bring our own luggage with us when we are faced with challenges in children's behaviour.

Have you ever heard yourself speaking to a child, only to realise that this was your own parents' voice to you when *you* were a child, spoken in the same tone and repeating the same phrases in the same kind of situation? Have you wondered why certain children's behaviours seem to strike to your very core and generate a fear or rage reaction in you, only to realise later that this is a shadow of something that happened to you in the past? We need not be ruled by our pasts, but having a grasp of where this emotional luggage comes from allows us to step back emotionally and deal with the situation more objectively. Our emotional luggage, once we have taken the time to unpack it a little, can actually make us more sensitive to what is going on in a child's own life.

Dealing with tantrums

As one of the most stressful behaviours we have to deal with, temper tantrums deserve a special mention. Temper tantrums are like intense storms of feeling and can be as alarming for a young child as they can be to us when having to deal with them. Although it might feel to you at the time that tantrums are all about battles for power, they can also be about genuine emotional pain.

Margot Sunderland (2007) describes two different types of tantrum, the 'distress' tantrum and what she terms as the 'little Nero' tantrum. With the former, you can see real anguish and pain in the child's face, and you need to handle it more sensitively. Use simple, calm actions, try distraction, talk gently (it will be your tone that gets through rather than your actual words at this point), stay close and use 'time in' rather than 'time out' approaches.

With the little Nero tantrums, you need to move away from the child and, having ensured that no one is in danger, cut back your attention until the tantrum is burning out. Once you give in to these kinds of tantrums, you have rewarded them, and they are likely to increase. Instead, reduce the audience if you can; avoid reasoning, argument, negotiation or persuasion and (as a last resort) try a time-out technique.

Temper tantrums

Pen picture

Marissa is two and has, on average, seven major temper tantrums per session. She presents as an angry little girl who finds it hard to wait for attention, share adult attention with other children and comply with requests. Staff members are worried that she is her own worst enemy – as soon as there is an interesting activity to do, Marissa appears to spoil it with her temper. They are concerned that she is not getting as much out of her nursery sessions as she could, and they are also concerned because of the effect her tantrums have on other children. They are finding it all extremely stressful.

How staff worked out what to do

Members of staff used one of their regular staff meetings to discuss Marissa's behaviour. They realized that this was far more than a passing phase and that they needed to plan approaches that were different to usual. They also realized the effect that the tantrums were having on their own emotions – with behaviour like this, the temptation is to feel angry in response and to see the child as being naughty. Talking to one another helped them to feel less angry and powerless themselves and see Marissa's behaviour more objectively. They agreed that Marissa needed to learn that temper tantrums did not lead to the desired result (more adult attention and/or getting her own way) and that she also needed to learn that playing socially could be fun and to learn the social skills that went with this. They suspected that Marissa was also an emotionally needy little girl who genuinely required a lot of support and attention. Talking together enabled staff to agree in precise words what constituted a temper tantrum for Marissa (screaming, falling down and kicking) and what observations they would gather (STAR observation – Chapter 6 – both for temper tantrums but also gathering information about activities that went really positively). They also talked with foster parents.

What they did

The period of observation turned out to be really important as the observer began to tune in to Marissa, her strong emotions and her frustrations. It seemed that she had genuine difficulties in accepting rules and guidelines. It was as if Marissa did not trust the adults around her to be consistent and that she needed to take control herself instead. This was scary for her. From what little the staff knew of her home background (she had recently been taken into foster care), this could well be the

(Continued)

(*Continued*)

case. Staff chose one of them to be a secure base for Marissa, greeting her each morning and spending individual time with her before joining the group and supporting her. Outbursts were treated consistently with calm containment – removing her calmly and firmly from the group whilst her key person sat silently with her until the outburst had subsided. She was then helped to rejoin the group and supported in a new activity.

Why it worked

The new, more sympathetic, way of regarding Marissa's outbursts helped staff members deal with them in a much calmer and more consistent way. There are some children who have developed unusual or disordered ways of forming emotional attachments (Chapter 1), and they tend to move rapidly from calm to extreme outburst with no shades of grey in between, as if they have learned that only a severe outburst of emotion is going to secure for them what they need. With the presence in her life of calm, consistent adults who could cope with and contain her outbursts, Marissa began to settle in the group and with her foster family, though it took some time.

Strategies for managing your own stress

There are certain self-help strategies that you can use in an attempt to remain calm and clear-thinking when working with challenging behaviour becomes tough:

- Start by evaluating how stressed you feel, either by trying the questionnaire below or talking with your peers or manager.
- If you know that a session is going to be particularly stressful, plan ahead by allowing yourself a five-minute time-out when you need to, with a colleague stepping in.
- Regulate your breathing to help you remain calm and clear-thinking.
- Try to set up a work-free zone in your setting where staff can relax – even if it is a quiet armchair with a Please Do Not Disturb sign!
- Remember that you do not need to be perfect – just professional and well informed.
- Agree with your manager or SENCO clear strategies for managing a child's disruptive behaviours when they occur so that you have a pre-agreed, regular routine to switch into.
- Switch into observer role so that you are watching the situation unfold through a professional lens; this can save you feeling too emotionally involved.
- Remember at all times that you are aiming to manage the behaviour and not the child.

- Keep records of all challenging times, but link these into your reflections and what you will try to do to make the situation better.
- Keep records of that child's 'ta-da!' moments too (Chapter 2) – these remind you why you have chosen the job that you so enjoy doing.
- If you were not sure what to do about a child's behaviour, ask for support.
- Hold regular get-togethers after a difficult session to debrief and unwind – then try to leave the issues behind you as you go home.
- Make sensitive use of humour to lighten the day, remaining professional and discreet.
- Have a bank of favourite 'chill' activities to dip into after work.

Coping with stress whilst managing behaviour

Circle **5** if you strongly agree
    4 if you generally agree
    3 if you don't know
    2 if you do not agree
    1 if you strongly disagree

I really enjoy working with young children.
5   4   3   2   1

I feel well-informed about understanding why children behave in the way that they do.
5   4   3   2   1

I can usually work out how to manage tricky behaviour.
5   4   3   2   1

It is fine to share problems concerning children's difficult behaviour with my manager/SENCO.
5   4   3   2   1

On most days I feel stressed and anxious at work.
5   4   3   2   1

I blame myself when things go wrong.
5   4   3   2   1

(*Continued*)

(Continued)

> How does stress affect you? (tick)
> Feeling shaky   Problems sleeping   Eating issues
> Problems concentrating   Opting out of situations Problems relaxing
> Thoughts keep going round in my head   Feeling sick
>
> Now think of three ideas that you will try to reduce your stress levels:
> 1
>
> 2
>
> 3

Talking with parents or carers about behaviour

It is one thing to share expectations of the children's behaviour and progress with your colleagues. It is another thing to work in partnership with parents and carers to establish a common language and expectation about their children's behaviour. How can you share your own expectations between home and setting? Look for opportunities to share with parents and carers what activities you are doing in the session and why – this all helps to give them clearer expectations about what stage their child has reached; for example, 'Young children have to be taught how to share, so we play simple turn-taking games to make this fun'; 'Most children use silly words if they notice people paying them attention; that is why you will find us ignoring some words they say'. Use positive questioning to find out the parents' or carers' views on the problem:

- 'How do you feel he is doing in the group?'
- 'What's going well?'
- What's her favourite thing here?'
- 'When does he behave best?'
- What helps her do that?'
- 'What do you think would make a difference in his behaviour in the group?'

Be aware of any cultural or religious reasons why parents and carers might view a behaviour problem differently from you. For example, parents might feel that it is right for their child to hit another child back or wrong for their child to join in a physical game. Respect the framework they are using and explain clearly what you need to achieve in the setting, seeking a mutually agreed compromise if necessary. Encourage visits to the group by parents and carers so that they can see how you manage a behaviour, and use it to explain why, without suggesting that parents are bad parents if they are not doing the same thing.

What if a child's behaviour is challenging at home, but you have no such issues within the setting? Having read this book, you will know that there is a myriad of reasons why this might be so. Explain to parents that children can learn to behave very differently in different situations; this avoids giving the impression that you are managing the behaviour in the setting because you are skilled and parents are not. You might then ask if there are concerns that they have about their child's behaviour which you might work together on. If a parent or carer sees a problem behaviour as a problem child and is very negative about their child, patiently rephrase the statements in terms of what the child is *doing* (rather than what they *are*). You can also plan interventions to support family relationships (Chapter 1) and work on how they view and relate to their child. Plan events where you can talk about a particular aspect of your play and behaviour policy together, so that you are all informed with the same knowledge of ages and stages.

This does not always go smoothly, and much will depend on the positive relationship you have already been able to form with parents and carers, long before you had to share the challenges. If there is an entrenched problem with a child's behaviour, make sure that you involve parents and carers from the early stages and involve them in your planning and consultation. If there are entrenched problems in communicating with

Thinking point

Suppose Mo has been in your setting for two terms and his behaviour has been very difficult to manage; he gets very excitable and can lash out at other children if he feels at all thwarted. You have been meeting with his mother regularly, though she has said very little. You have reached the point where you would like to seek outside professional help. Mo's mother looks doubtful and says she would need to talk with her partner. His father then comes in very angry and tells you that all Mo needs is sound disciplining. He adds, 'There's no way he's going to see anyone else as there's nothing wrong with his head'.

Things to consider:

- What do you do?
- What emotions might be underlying Dad's reactions?
- How could you work towards bringing him on board?
- Would it ever be appropriate to involve an outside agency without parental consent?

You will find a bank of helpful suggestions in the section 'Useful approaches'.

parents and carers, keep a record of what you have tried and talk to outside professionals in an attempt to look for creative and innovative ways through. Remember that safeguarding and child protection procedures are of paramount importance. Make links with any local support services so that you can work together on the expectations which local families and carers have of their young children. Above all, share the pleasures of the caring as well as the problems. Show that you like and respect their child and build on the fact that you both wish the best for that child.

Understanding where parents and carers might be coming from

It is not easy talking with a parent or carer about their child's behaviour. There are all sorts of emotions which can be aroused, and it helps if you can tune in to some of the emotional reactions which the child might be picking up from a parent.

Guilt

Parents might be wondering what they did wrong, or feeling that you are blaming them in some way for the fact that their child has a behaviour problem. It helps to emphasise how much you value parents' help and advice in helping *you* manage the difficulty for their child. 'Thank you so much for coming to talk. We are having some difficulties in managing Tara's temper tantrums. It's clear that she gets quite upset with us all and we are keen to make her sessions happier for her. You know her better than anyone, so it will be really useful to talk'.

Blame

Parents may find it easiest to blame other people for the problem – perhaps even suggesting that their child learned to swear or become aggressive from the setting. They may report that there are no such problems at home and so the problem must lie in the way staff are managing the problem. It might help to comment, 'That's interesting that there are no problems like this at home. I wonder if she only behaves like this when she has to do something she doesn't want to or when there are lots of other children around – like when she is expected to share the toys here?' Parents and carers may also have rigid ideas about discipline and blame you for not having the same ideas ('All he needs is a good ___!'). It helps to explain clearly what you are allowed to do and what not and explain why. 'The law does not allow us to smack your child. This is because we now know that smacking encourages children to hurt others, and we have to treat children with the same respect as we would anyone else. It is also our policy to use positive approaches which will help your child's emotional development in the long term'.

Protectiveness

Parents and carers may jump to their child's defence. They may also feel that they have made a mistake in sending their child to you and that you might not be able to cope with their child as they have. They may also find it hard to share the responsibility of their child's behaviour with you in the setting and therefore to lose control of what is happening. A 'no blame' problem-solving approach works best in which you make it clear that it is the *behaviour* which is the problem and not the child: for example, 'We would like to work with you to change Kerry's behaviour. What do *you* think will work best?'

Anger

People whose self-esteem is low, who feel threatened in some way or who have had negative experiences of professional power may become quickly angry. Look after your own safety (your professional organization should have guidelines for you). It also helps to have established a working relationship with parents long before you are in the position of having to share any 'bad news'. In this way, you cease to become a threat because you are someone who is already accepted and trusted.

Grief

Sometimes you might raise a fairly minor behaviour problem with a parents or carer only to be taken by surprise by an outpouring of grief. You can never know where someone's emotions come from and there may be good reasons why this is happening. Other parents may avoid even meeting you or talking about the problem because they are not sure how they will cope. It helps to allow plenty of time to work through any emotion and address all concerns in a practical and helpful way.

Anxiety

Some parents and carers may appear overly anxious about their child. They may have their own difficulties in separating from their child and find it hard to trust you. Where possible, make sure that the parent and child have had initial visits before the child starts with you. Once the child attends regularly, handle the separation confidently and firmly, distracting the child into play with their key person. Later, find a way to reassure the parent that all went well.

Rejection of the problem

Parents and carers may feel that they don't want to be the sort of people who have this sort of child, and so they act as if there is nothing to be concerned about. Sometimes this gets bound in with rejection of any kind of label and an expressed wish that their child should not be treated any differently from the other children. It helps if you can make it clear that you are not keen to label the child but that you are very keen to help the child behave more appropriately and become a happy, socially adjusted individual.

Helplessness and denial

Sometimes when family members are stressed or depressed, you may find avoidance or denial from parents and carers: 'I'm rushing off and can't talk', 'It will all be all right', 'He's just like Uncle Dennis was' or 'It's just the way she is'. Other parents and carers may be out of tune with their child's difficulties, perhaps because child and parent are 'unconnected' or have attachment difficulties (Chapter 1). In this situation, it can appear to you as if they simply do not care.

Useful approaches

So how can a sensitivity to the underlying emotions help you approach a parent or carer about their child's behaviour? These approaches were worked out by a large workshop of over a hundred early years practitioners on a study day that we held on young children's behaviour (Mortimer, 2006).

- Try to understand why a parent or carer might be saying something. What does this tell you all about their emotional state and how you might help?
- If there is avoidance of the issue, try to take time to share the good news of progress before you need to share the challenges. Give clear information about your expectations in order to inform a parent about what you hope to achieve at each age and stage. This will lead on to what you are going to plan together for those areas that are showing a weakness.
- Involve parents and carers in the sessions wherever possible so they can *see* what you are trying to achieve. Try not just to share the activities but to share the reasoning behind them and an idea of how children typically progress. Try to share some of your enthusiasm in the way children play and learn and to pass on skills.
- For helpless or troubled parents, try to give practical workable advice, but try not to give the impression that you are the successful ones and parents are failing; parents with low self-esteem are quick to pick up the fact that they are 'not doing it right'. This leads to resentfulness and avoidance. Instead, negotiate any home-setting activities and be encouraging and warm: for example, 'What seems to keep his attention at home?', 'What do you find works best when she behaves like this?', 'When do you find he behaves best?' or 'What help do you need from us?'
- If a parent or carer denies there is anything wrong, start with where they are at in terms of their understanding, but make it clear what might happen next: for example, 'I'm glad you're not worried about her. But we must teach her to sit and listen in the group, even if she's fine at home, because she needs to be able to do this by the time she starts school. So perhaps we can talk about what seems to work at home and we'll put together a plan to teach her to concentrate here. As you say, she may settle

very quickly. If not, we'll talk again next term and plan what to do next.' Be firm, stick to your plan and continue to involve parents and carers with every sign of progress or need, making it clear that you are doing this in order to keep them in touch.

- If a parent won't stop to talk, negotiate a home visit to meet on their territory. Start with establishing *their* views and feelings; this gives you important information about their value judgements which will help you decide how to introduce your own concerns. Listen first, talk later, find the common ground last. The common ground is usually your mutual like of their child who is special to both of you.
- If parents appear overly anxious, try to take their views seriously and, point by point, reassure with concrete evidence that all is well.
- Wherever possible, give parents a job to do: suggestions for home are an excellent starting point.
- What if other parents are discriminating? 'If that child continues to attend, I'll take mine away'. This is a direct challenge to your Special Needs and Equal Opportunities policy, goes against the spirit of the SEN Disability Act and can't be fudged, though you might well understand the parents' fears or state of misinformation. Explain that it is your policy to welcome all children regardless of special need. State clearly what steps you are taking (in general terms rather than personal details) to make sure the other children's needs are not compromised.
- Consider arranging a session for everyone on managing difficult behaviour or rising to the challenge – usually *every* parent and carer (and professional!) has their challenging moments at some stage and this can be a very levelling and unifying experience for everyone.
- In the boxed section, you will find a crib sheet to photocopy for handing to parents if you need to provide general guidelines. You can suggest that these approaches are tried first, offering to talk more after three weeks if parents do not feel they are getting anywhere.

Encouraging good behaviour at home

- Praise your child frequently and straightaway if the child is behaving appropriately.
- It is best if you do not spend time cross-examining the child as to *why* they did something; your child might not always know, and it can hurt sensitive feelings.
- Stick to routines. This provides predictability for your child and means that there is less to remember.
- Say your child's name, get down to her level, keep instructions clear and offer one at a time.

(Continued)

(Continued)

- Stay calm and do not become heated when dealing with difficult behaviour – this is like fanning the flames of the fire and only makes things worse.
- In the heat of a moment, do not spend time reasoning or negotiating; be calm, clear, firm and predictable. You can talk about things later when everything is calm again.
- Avoid difficult times and plan around them (such as not taking your child to a crowded supermarket unless it cannot be avoided).
- Do not use physical punishment. It does not work effectively and can actually make your child's behaviour more aggressive in the long term.
- Take one day at a time; tomorrow is another day!

Home-setting liaison

If you are going to have effective and productive liaison between home and setting, then you need to look at proactive ways of making this happen. First, you need to build up a basic respect for each other. You hope that parents and carers will acknowledge that you have something positive to offer their children. You in turn need to acknowledge the fundamental role that parents or carers have already played in their child's education. Look for ways of sharing the learning between home and setting by providing regular information, updating your website, e-mails and newsletters.

Make sure that parents and carers feel welcome in your setting and that there are opportunities for working together. Make your admission procedures flexible to allow time for discussion with parents and carers and for children to feel secure in a new setting. If you already have an ongoing relationship with parents, then it makes it so much easier to talk about problems if and when they arise.

Home programmes

One useful way of supporting parents or carers of a child with behaviour difficulties is to negotiate a 'play plan' to share with them. This contains ideas for supporting their child's learning and behaviour at home and it can link in with the child's individual behaviour plan (Chapter 6). Be sensitive to the language in which parents usually communicate, and use an interpreter if you need to, or even consider a project for linking parents and carers together for support.

The following example is a play plan for Robbie, a little boy who finds it hard to concentrate for long on any one activity. The main section is shared with parents or carers, who take it home and try out the ideas. The last section has their comments on how well

Play Plan for *Robbie*

Play helps *Robbie* **to** *look, listen and concentrate.*

Getting Started
Help Robbie to play for longer with you. Let him choose what he wants to play with and you play with him too for at least ten minutes each early evening. Play somewhere where it is quiet and there are not too many distractions. Do it when his little sister is in bed. Give lots of praise and show him how pleased you are.

When you need to speak to him, say his name and go up to him. Ask him to look at you. Say it very simply (2 or 3 words at the most). If he still does not listen, go with him and help him do what you have asked. Again, praise him warmly.

Games to Play
1. *Construction and car games: using bricks and fitting pieces which Robbie can easily manage.*
2. *Give Robbie a chart to show how many times he listened to what you said. Add a sticker to it for each success.*
3. *Point out interesting things to see on bus journeys and walks.*
4. *Share picture books together – we will lend you some.*

How to help
As Robbie becomes more able to concentrate, reduce the amount of help you give until he is managing to play a little bit all by himself, so long as you are nearby.

How did *Robbie* get on?
Monday
He played with his cars for five minutes with me without throwing them at me!
Tuesday
Today Robbie managed to watch his favourite programme on TV without fighting with his sister.
Thursday
We had a dreadful day. I still think that he reacts badly to what he's eating. Who can I talk to about this?

Robbie managed the tasks, which they bring back to share with the setting. Alternatively, you can complete this section together when you meet parents again for feedback.

Parents and carers might also find it helpful to contact a support group for more help or information. If appropriate, think of accessible information, pamphlets and websites which are helpful for parents or carers as well as for early years practitioners. Think of books which you can share with the children too; these can provide starting points for talking about the child's own views, feelings and wishes; there are some suggestions at the end of the chapter.

Support services

In a changing climate, it is impossible to describe categorically what support services might be available and who to turn to for external professional help, and you would be advised to contact your local children's services agency to find out more. There is so much variation between regions and countries. The important thing to remember is that time with a young child is precious and soon passes. We can never put a halt on our interventions and support whilst we wait for something to happen or, for example, 'wait to see if it's AD/HD or ASD'. We ourselves are professionals in how children develop, learn, thrive and behave. Whilst we exist within wider support networks, we are the ones, along with parents and carers, with day-to-day influence on the child's emotional development and well-being. It is our duty to plan, do, evaluate, review and keep records so that we can paint a picture of that child and the interventions that appear to be effective when it comes to any wider professional involvement later on. Either your approaches will work, or the monitoring that you have done will provide important 'evidence' for any future referral to an outside professional. You *must* have faith that interventions in early years manifestly *do* work – and how rewarded you will feel when your detective work has achieved the positive changes that you hoped for. We have said before that time in early years is precious; we must use it well!

References

Mortimer, H. (2006) *Behaviour Management in the Early Years*. Stafford: QEd Publications.
Sunderland, M. (2007) *What Every Parent Needs to Know*. London: Dorling Kindersley.

Books to encourage talking and listening around feelings

- *The Best-Loved Bear* by Diana Noonan and Elizabeth Fuller (Scholastic)
- *Scared of a Bear* by Hilda Offen (Hodder Children's Books)
- *No Worries!* by Marcia Williams (Walker Books)
- *The Good Mood Hunt* by Hiawyn Oram and Joanne Partis (Oxford University Press)
- *Hug* by Jez Alborough (Walker Books)

- *I Love Hugs* by Lara Jones (Scholastic)
- *When Sophie Gets Angry – Really, Really Angry* by Molly Garrett (Scholastic)
- *The Huge Bag of Worries* by Virginia Ironside (Hodder)
- *Mad Isn't Bad: A Child's Book about Anger* by Michaeline Mundy (Abbey Press)

The Magination Press (www.apa.org/pubs/magination) specialises in books which help young children deal with personal or psychological concerns.

Further information

For information on current **guidance and statutory requirements in the UK**, visit the standard Early Years Government websites:

- For England: https://www.gov.uk/early-years-foundation-stage
- For Scotland: http://www.gov.scot/Topics/People/Young-People/early-years/delivery/framework
- For Wales: http://gov.wales/topics/educationandskills/earlyyearshome/foundation-phase/?lang=en
- For Northern Ireland: https://www.nidirect.gov.uk/articles/early-years-teams

For further information on your **local support services**, visit the website for your Local Authority Children's Services.

Index

additives 52
anger 7, 16, 32, 37, 39, 51, 82, 105, 113, 119
anti-social behaviour 14
anxiety 5, 11, 16, 32–3, 37, 48, 51, 87, 90, 94, 98, 105, 109, 113, 115
appropriate behaviour xi, xiii, 14–5, 26, 29–30, 34–5, 45–6, 49–51, 53–4, 59–60, 63–5, 67, 69, 74, 76, 78, 80–3, 87, 113, 115
arousal system 3, 52–3
assertiveness 21, 24, 49
assessment xii, 31, 70–2, 87, 89
attachment
   ambivalent 5
   anxious-avoidant 5
   difficulties 5–6, 87, 114
   disorganized 5
   function of 4
   patterns of 5–6
   secure base 5–8, 14, 28, 31, 33, 56, 108
   positive attachments 3, 7–14, 30
attention
   deficit/hyperacticity disorder (AD/HD) 16, 85, 87, 89, 98–103, 118
   development of 20–21, 49, 62, 68–9
   difficulties xv, 16, 77–9, 82–3, 98–103, 107
   -seeking 82–3
Autistic Spectrum Disorder (ASD) xv, 22, 57, 75, 85–98, 118

Ballard, J. 33
behaviour consultation 83–5
behaviour detective xii, xiv, 3, 77, 105
behaviour management xiii, xv, 30, 44, 64, 66, 72–83, 85, 102, 118
behaviour policy xv, 51, 62–7, 111

behaviour support teacher 65, 69
Bennathan and Boxhall 10
bereavement 36–9
biting 69, 76, 81–2
blame 109, 112–3
boredom 2–3, 53
bossiness 20–1
boundary setting xiv, 14, 29, 34, 53, 59, 61, 68, 77, 80, 101
brain development xiv, 1–3, 51, 67, 87–8, 90, 105
Brodie, K. 40
broken record technique 46, 79, 97

CAMHS (Child and Adolescent Mental Health Service) 39, 85
child development xii–xv, 2, 4, 14–28, 51, 53, 59, 68, 78, 81, 87–9, 92, 98, 118
childminding xii, 72
circle time 21, 23–25, 27, 31, 33, 43, 56, 63, 65, 68–9, 79, 103
Clark and Moss 41
'clear and cloudy' statements 44–5
comforter 7
communication
   development of 22
   difficulties 6, 88–98
concentration 20, 62–3, 80, 101
confidence
   in children xii, xiv, 11–12, 17, 20–21, 23–25, 28–32, 34, 45, 63, 65, 68, 77, 99
   in adults 43, 62, 73, 77, 82, 91, 104–5
   in yourself xiv, 25, 28, 68–9
consequences approach 14, 18, 40, 46, 60, 70–4, 80–3

Index

consistency 5, 7, 14, 18, 35, 39, 75, 80–1, 102, 107–8
consultation
 with children 40–2
 with each other xv, 83–5
 with parents and carers 66, 111
crying 2–3, 5, 11–12, 38
culture xiii, 17, 19, 42

denial 114
diet 48, 52
discipline 13–14, 112
Drummond, Rouse and Pugh xiii

early years practitioners xi, xii, 4, 16, 86, 114, 117
egocentricity 17
emotional development xiv, 1, 6–14, 28–39, 112, 118
emotional literacy 39, 106
emotional luggage xv, 106
ethnicity xiii, 17, 39, 42, 59
expectations xiv, 14, 18, 29, 33–34, 44, 49, 51, 54–5, 59, 78, 87, 89, 92, 110, 112, 114
exploration
 in children xi–xii, xiv, 2, 4, 20, 28, 30, 42, 44, 53
 and attachment 4
 and play 28, 53
 when adults are planning 83–4, 105

feeding 19
fight or flight reaction 1, 3
friendships xiv, 6, 13, 17–18, 29, 32, 45, 65, 80

game plan 96
Gardner, H. 25
gender xiii, 17, 39, 59
gifted and talented 25–7
Gray, Carol 96
grieving 36–9, 113
guilt 104, 112

higher brain 2, 14, 22
home programme 116–7
home-setting liaison 116

inappropriate behaviour xi, xv, 18, 51, 60, 63, 67–8, 74, 79, 81, 96
indirect statements 47
individual behaviour plan xii, xv, 59, 65, 68–70, 116
individual differences 26–7

intelligence
 emotional 31–32, 39, 106
 interpersonal 25
 intrapersonal 25
 multiple 25, 39
 quotient (IQ) 25–26, 31
intuition xi

Jordan, R. 88

key person 3–5, 7–11, 28, 31, 33, 36–7, 48, 54, 56, 62, 68–9, 95, 108
Kohlberg 18

labeling conditions xv, 6, 44, 86–7, 98, 113
language development 13, 40, 42–3

mammalian brain 2
Mayer and Salovey, 32
mediation 47
metaphors xiv, 40, 42–3, 47–8
moral development 18, 25, 27
Mortimer, H. xii, 23, 24, 90, 114
mosaic approach 41, 50
Mosley, J. 33
motivation 25, 29, 32, 45, 60, 63, 74, 97, 101
multi-sensory approaches 55, 79
musical circle time ('Musicmakers') xiv, 21, 23–5
musical interaction 90

nurture
 corners 7, 10, 33
 groups 10, 14

observation xv, 18, 37, 46, 67–72, 81, 93, 100, 102, 107

pacifier 42
parent support xii, xv, 5, 9, 62, 76–7, 87, 102–4, 110–8
peer praise 49
personal and social development xi, 15–27
picture exchange (PECS) 94
picture timetables 34, 57, 79, 92
Portage 45, 77
positive
 attachments 3, 7–14, 30
 attention 6, 78
 feedback 49
 expectations 34, 49
 mental health 4
 relationships 15, 17, 111
 self-esteem 17, 39, 45, 76

122

Index

positive approaches xi, xiii, xv, 1, 6, 8, 30, 39, 46, 48, 51, 55, 63–66, 73–4, 80, 102, 110, 112
practitioners xi, xii, 2, 4, 16, 18–19, 23–4, 86–87, 89, 105, 114, 117
problem-solving 2, 20–1, 26, 47, 83, 113
protectiveness 112–3, 4, 17
psychologist xii, 10, 24, 31, 76, 85
psychology 41, 73, 119
puppet play 21, 37, 43, 58

relationship circle 7–10
relationships
  vertical 17
  horizontal 17
religion xiii, 38–9, 59, 110
reptilian brain 1
rewards 72–5, 97, 102
'right and wrong' 18, 32, 35
risk
  assessment 62, 80
  and resilience 6, 10
role models 63, 90
room management 54
routines xiv, 5, 7, 34–5, 37, 52–3, 56, 67, 79, 88–9, 95, 101, 115
rules xiv, 14, 18, 22, 34, 40, 45, 49, 54, 59, 62, 65, 67–8, 79, 82, 89, 94, 107
rules-praise-ignore 49

safeguarding procedures 57, 68, 111
scripts, development of 46, 93
secure base 5–8, 14, 28, 31, 33, 56, 108
security xi, xiv, 1, 3–9, 17, 20, 28–31, 33–4, 39, 51, 53, 56–7, 60–2, 80, 89, 94–5, 108, 116
self-confidence xiv, 25, 28, 68–9
self-discipline 35, 54
self-esteem xiii–xiv, 6, 14, 29–31–4, 45–6, 63, 68–9, 74, 99, 104, 113–4
SEN (special educational needs) xii, xv, 55, 87–8
SENCO (special educational needs coordinator) xii, 30, 64, 69, 83, 85, 108–9
SEN and disabilities (SEND) xv, 56–7, 86
separation distress 2, 5–6, 11, 31, 37
shaping 19, 46, 59–61
sleep, effect on behaviour xiv, 36, 51–3, 110
social
  behaviour xi–xii, 15–27, 68, 86
  communication 22, 96

independence 17, 19, 23, 60
interaction 15, 33, 87, 94, 97
play 71, 82, 102, 107
praise 6, 8, 12, 14, 21, 29, 31, 46, 49, 65, 68, 70, 74–5, 78, 80–2, 97, 100–2, 115, 117
signals 96
skills xiv, 14, 16–20, 23, 25, 32, 51, 65, 74, 80–1, 86, 90, 94, 96, 100, 102, 107
worlds 111, 15, 18, 20, 67
social skills training 80, 94, 96
social stories 96, 103
social worker 76, 85
socio-economic disadvantage 6
special playtime 7–8
speech and language therapist 24, 42, 87
STAR chart
  observation chart 69, 70–1
  reward system 83
statutory guidance xiii, 120
strength-based approaches xiv, 1, 12, 14, 89–93, 99–100
stress
  management 104–6, 108–10
  response 3, 35–6, 57
Sunderland, Margot 1, 52, 66, 106
support
  for parents and carers xii, xv, 5, 9, 62, 76–7, 87, 102–4, 110–8
  services 78, 112, 118, 120
sustained shared thinking 40, 50

'ta-da!' moments xiv, 22–3, 92, 101, 109
temperament xiv, 6, 26–7
temper tantrums 57, 71, 74, 106–8, 112
therapeutic support 4, 9, 33, 37–9, 48, 55
time-out 61, 106, 108
toilet-training 19, 47–8
traffic lights 61
transition
  objects 12, 34, 95
  between situations xv, 10, 12, 37, 57–8, 63, 78
trauma xiv, 6, 35–8, 58
triad of (autistic) impairments 88–9

visualization 34
voluntary organizations xii

warnings 49, 78, 98